The Great Truth

Shattering Life's Most
Insidious Lies That
Sabotage Your Happiness
Along With The Revelation
of Life's Sole Purpose

JANET PFEIFFER

BALBOA.
PRESS

A DIVISION OF HAY HOUSE

ISBN: 978-1-4525-5607-9 (sc)
ISBN: 978-1-4525-5608-6 (e)
Library of Congress Control Number: 2012913481

Balboa Press books may be ordered through booksellers or by contacting:

Balboa Press
A Division of Hay House
1663 Liberty Drive
Bloomington, IN 47403
www.balboapress.com
1-(877) 407-4847

The names and situations in this book have sometimes been changed
to protect the privacy of those involved. Many of the examples given
are my own personal experiences presented as though they have
happened to others. This was done to protect those who wish to remain
anonymous. As for me, I have never had a problem revealing the ugly
truth about myself. I firmly believe others can learn from me either by
the example I set or by the mistakes I've made. Being brutally honest
with myself is only half the challenge. Exposing my imperfections
to others is cathartic for me and hopefully beneficial to others.

Printed in the United States of America

Balboa Press rev. date: 09/07/2012

Your life "has everything to do with _____!" So, how would you fill in the blank? Janet Pfeiffer's latest book provides the answer. If you're wondering about the mystery of the human experience, wonder no longer. Instead, read this remarkable book by an equally remarkable person whose experiences throughout life have guided her to life's ultimate Mystery and Meaning. Again, Janet, you have demonstrated, not only your expertise as a writer, but your insights into life, happiness, purpose and meaning.

- Dr. Steve McSwain, speaker, leadership coach, spiritual mentor, author of the award-winning book, The Enoch Factor: The Sacred Art of Knowing God

* * *

This book is a gem! It provides countless stories and examples of kindness and selflessness. It prompts you to reconsider how you move through life if it's not already in a way that promotes peace and benefits humanity. Janet shares a multitude of ways to create a more joyful and fulfilling life experience. It will fill you heart with wonder and you'll want to share it with the world!

- Leanne Kimble, owner, Canine Companions

* * *

Janet, what I like most is your honesty and willingness to share from the heart. Your spirit of joy comes through the pages. The heroic way you held on to our Lord's hand through the difficulties you endured and the very special way He touched you at your darkest moment is a great testimony so needed for our times. And your ability to love the one who hurt you most is your victory, thanks be to the grace of God.

I came away with an understanding that our lives really should center on our relationship with God and that the more we understand Him as He is - True Love - the better our lives and our relationships will be. And if we miss this reality we will be living a lie filled with sorrow.

Also, the danger of not accepting those for who they are really falls short of what God expects from His children, who are called to love as He loves.

Your message resonates with each of us and I look forward to recommending your book to others.

- Phil Brady, Pastoral Assoiciate, Founder, Migrant Relief Services, Workspace Wellness Designer

* * *

I really enjoyed reading The Great Truth: Shattering Life's Most Insidious Lies That Sabotage Your Happiness Along With The Revelation of Life's Sole Purpose. Your stories about the battered women you work with really touched my heart and shined light into the affectivness of your connection with both them and God. The story about your son retrieving his little sister's plastic ring was priceless! You have a way of making your readers laugh, cry, and search their souls for deeper awareness.

Thank you, Janet, for allowing your readers to understand that we are never alone, that our faith cannot grow without being tested, and that God truly has a Divine plan and purpose for each of us as we undertake this assignment called life.

- Michael J. DiNardo, singer, entertainer

This book is written with deep gratitude first and foremost to my Creator and Heavenly Father. My heart overflows with joy and love for you every moment of every day and for all you have and continue to bless me with. My greatest pleasure in life is in serving you.

Second, to my mother, Rae - my greatest example of God's perfect Love manifest in physical form. I aspire to be more like you every day.

Third, for my dear Moses, who despite the enormous challenges that plague his life, continue to love and serve the Father through his kind and generous heart.

This book is written in loving memory of my dad, Clayton Lewis Pfeiffer.

Contents

Foreword

by Bernie Siegel, MD

Due to the fact that they are raised without love most people don't know what to do with life. They live in a state of ego and self-interest due to their feeling rejected - "I want to meet the right person and get married." "I'm going to fulfill my life-long dream." "I'm going to travel around the world and experience life to the fullest!" They do not view any of those things as enhancing the life of anyone else. A life centered on the self is shallow and unrewarding and is not really about choosing life but about self-interest. And yet due to what the authority figures in our life have taught us most of us have been indoctrinated to believe this is the way of life.

Some come to the realization that a life of fulfillment centers on helping others. While this can certainly add greater meaning and depth to our lives, it can sometimes lead to disappointment and resentment when we did not make this choice out of love and efforts go unrecognized by others. When we act out of love a reward is not necessary.

Then there are those who adopt a philosophy of doing what makes them happy. "Surely, that is the key to our existence." Yet happiness is but a fleeting moment if it is related only to the individual's desires but if it is to make the world a happier place then everyone is rewarded.

In The Great Truth Janet eloquently shares her journey of realizing that her life is not about herself, her family or even her career. The discovery of this Truth dramatically alters the manner in which she lives her life and when applied, removes all resistance to what is, alleviates suffering and despair, and replaces it with a lasting sense of appreciation, joy, and harmony with all.

The great Holy Books, including the Bible, the Bhagavad Gita, the Tripitaka, and others, all speak of the nature of the Divine. The Gita discusses the exact process by which human beings can establish their eternal relationship with God and attain oneness with the Him. The Gita says, "The One I love is incapable of ill will and returns love for hatred. Living beyond the reach of I and mine, and of pain and pleasure, full of mercy, contented, self-controlled, of firm resolve, with all His heart and all His mind has given to me – with such a One I am in love."

Janet's latest book contains a series of her own meditative reflections on life and meaning which give one much food-for-thought on living life with love, compassion, forgiveness, courage, and deep faith immersed in the Spirit of God.

Her stories illuminate authentic lessons one must incorporate into their daily routines in order to live the message they share each day. She skillfully lays out the lifelong, common sense blueprint anyone can follow which will ultimately align their heart with that of the Divine.

As God said to me on one of my visits to Heaven, "When you graduate from school you call it a commencement, not a termination, and the Bible ends in Revelations not conclusions. So life is a series of beginnings."

Join Janet as she guides you in beginning a new and more profound way of living. Experience the revelation of The Great Truth and, as she so poignantly states it, "falling in love with God all over again for the first time".

All books of wisdom are meant to be read more than once. This is one such book and you will become wiser each time you read it because you are learning and growing from the experience it provides.

Introduction

What if everything you believed about life was a lie? That's a pretty unsettling question. We've all grown up with myriad beliefs and clichés that have paved the roads we traverse. We were taught to set goals for ourselves and strive to achieve them. Each success bolstered our self-esteem and raised our status among our family members, peers, and society. Whether in the form of degrees received, dollars earned, titles bestowed, awards and trophies won, weight lost, records held, followers on Facebook and Twitter, and such, it's easy to get caught up in the dictates of societal standards.

Each generation and culture has their own set of unique beliefs that define who they are and the way they live their lives. Many of us have been instructed to follow our dreams, do what makes us happy, not worry about what others think about us (after all, our opinion is all that really matters, right?), and live in the moment. We're taught that failure is not an option, that we should be the best and succeed at all costs, that all's fair in love and war, and so on. Some are told to be grateful. Others are advised that one can't ever be too thin or too rich, and that younger is better, and so is bigger. We make sure no one gets away with anything and believe we have a right to teach others a lesson or get even, when necessary, with those who have wronged us. We shouldn't have to put up with nonsense from anyone and we should be exempt from injustice and hardship. We're encouraged to think about ourselves first and make sure we get what we rightfully deserve.

We feel justified in concerning ourselves with what others are doing even when it is none of our business. People from around the globe seek the *American Dream* (however that is currently defined). We search for someone to love who will reciprocate our affections. We strive to hold on to what belongs to us. We seek restitution when personal property is damaged, lost or stolen and make sure to replace it shortly thereafter. We become angry when things don't go our way and feel justified in labeling and judging others. We concern ourselves with prestige and status within our families, communities, place of employment, and society.

Some people aspire to achieve greatness, fame or fortune, to leave their mark on this world, and to set or break records. Work hard, retire, and then enjoy life - that's the American way.

There are many people who, perhaps after acquiring much, come to realize life is not about big houses, expensive cars, designer clothes, and so on. They have *seen the light* so-to-speak and discovered life is more about family, friends, good health, having fun, and helping others. And while the former brought them temporary pleasure, it failed to provide authentic happiness. This newer realization has proven much more fulfilling to them.

And still, very few people comprehend the true purpose of life. They continue to struggle and suffer in so many respects and believe that's just the way life is. Everything we strive to attain in life has the potential to disappoint us. Goals are thwarted by unforeseen circumstances, people let us down or outright betray us, unexpected hardships appear where clear sailing was predicted, limitations and setbacks disillusion us. We become disenchanted with life, ourselves, and those around us. There are no guarantees in life yet we hope and pray and plan for the best. When it is not forthcoming we feel frustrated, angry, and hopeless. The analogy of a salmon swimming upstream in a river only to die upon reaching his destination seems apropos for many of us.

We search to find meaning for our lives. Some determine life is about family, others believe it's about pursuing their dreams, and still others feel it is about helping one another or being happy. Then there are those who believe we are meant to fulfill our *divine destiny*.

The purpose of life is not what we have been led to believe.

Everything we have been taught has some degree of importance. Yet those elements that define who we are and what a successful, happy life consists of are tragically flawed. It is impossible to achieve absolute and permanent bliss, to feel completely and utterly satisfied and attain inner peace because our formula for life is erroneous. Thus, we remain in a constant state of turmoil and confusion.

It has taken me more than half a century to attain this profound awareness of life, to fully appreciate why I am here, and to redesign the way I live each day so as to be in perfect accordance with *sole purpose*.

Thank you for choosing to read my book. I promise you will not be disappointed. You are about to embark on a journey like none you've ever experienced before. Put aside all concerns of finding happiness, satisfying your dreams or being loved. *This* will replace all prior beliefs and needs and transform your life in ways unimaginable. You will discover an ease of living, be rewarded for every effort, and experience absolute fulfillment.

CHAPTER 1

My Way or the High Way

I Did It My Way

I've struggled considerably in life and made a lot of mistakes. I've always tried hard to be a good person, do the right thing, and make smart choices. But too often the decisions I made did not yield the results I had hoped for. In many instances they made matters worse, and in some cases, much worse. My self-esteem plummeted with every gaffe and guilt devoured me for the suffering I'd caused others.

My parents brought me up in the Catholic faith and taught me to live according to the Ten Commandments, even though they seemed rather rigid and sometimes incomplete in today's world. Adhering to them was like obeying the speed limit - necessary so one avoids getting in trouble with the law. Keeping myself and others safe seemed only a bi-product of civil obedience. Obeying God's command, even though intellectually knowing it was for my own good, was more an obligation than a concerned lifestyle choice. They also seemed rather simplistic, leaving a lot of circumstances open to individual interpretation which can have a disastrous outcome.

Old Blue Eyes

One of the most popular songs in musical history was recorded by old blue eyes himself, Mr. Frank Sinatra. "My Way" speaks of a life lived without regret. Maybe he was lucky or maybe the lyrics just made for great music. Either way, my life is filled with regrets. It's not so much for the missed opportunities - I can rationalize that at the moment they presented themselves perhaps I was not ready to take full advantage of them. Neither is it for the suffering I've caused myself - I can find value in knowing it has all been necessary for my personal growth. Each trauma, each injustice, and each betrayal taught me some of life's most valuable lessons and for that I am eternally grateful. But I do feel a deep sense of remorse for the times I've caused pain and suffering to others. And I've caused my share.

There is, in my mind, no justification for that - *ever.* There are many who would argue I did the best I could at the time. Really? If I am truly honest with myself, there were many times I did not do my best and I knew it. Sometimes I was too tired or I didn't care enough. Other times I was hurt or angry and disregarded how my behavior would affect those around me. And yes, I understand that I, like the rest of humanity, am imperfect and incapable of never faltering. But I'm very hard on myself and that's ok. It helps me maintain my personal standard of integrity and (hopefully) live my moral values.

I've never fared well with uncertainty and found myself thrust into a life laden with ambiguous questions in need of answers. I've worried about making wrong decisions and agonized over the unknown. When I was in college, I took a course on philosophy that was both fascinating and challenging. My professor was known for giving us controversial subjects to debate - abortion, the death penalty, and social and political issues. He'd assign half of the class to argue one side of the issue and the remaining students to take the opposing view. Regardless of our personal position, we had to research every aspect of the subject matter and present a valid and winning case. The purpose of such debates was not to prove one side right and the other wrong. His objective was to challenge us to think.

In any situation, the most valid and lasting judgments are drawn when each party carefully and thoroughly examines all facets of the issue before drawing a conclusion. Too often, we quickly form opinions about a subject or individual without fully investigating all the *Me* evidence and gaining as much knowledge and insights as possible. When such decisions are made in haste or without sufficient and unbiased knowledge, we form inaccurate conclusions with flawed results.

Making decisions in life can be daunting. It is often difficult (if not impossible) to fully realize if we have actually made the best decision possible. My choice may temporarily give me satisfaction but will it sustain the test of time? And has this decision proven beneficial not only to me but to those around me? It may appear to but how do I know for certain?

Not fully trusting in one's own ability, many of us seek the advice and guidance of others. Some turn to family members whom they respect and trust, others seek the esteemed knowledge and direction from trained professionals, such as therapists and pastors. Millions have chosen self-help books and life coaches to guide them with some of their most salient decisions.

Yet how do any of us know for certain if the advice we are given is correct? No matter how much experience my grandmother has, no matter how many degrees follow the name of my therapist, and no matter how many books my favorite self-help guru has written, aren't I relying on prejudicial advice?

Dog Bites and Divorce

In 1982, my first marriage abruptly came to a screeching halt. Without warning my husband unexpectedly announced he was leaving. Begging and pleading, I convinced him to accompany me to a marriage counselor - just once. It was my only hope of saving the marriage I was so deeply invested in.

With the help of a therapist I knew and trusted, I acquired the name of a professional and promptly made an appointment. With great trepidation, we set out on a Thursday evening for our 7:00 appointment. I quickly summarized our thirteen-year marriage and what I perceived to be the necessary issues to address. The therapist listened and asked relevant questions. Then, without warning, he began to speak exclusively to my husband about moving on and finding someone new. (Had I suddenly become invisible?) "Why stay in a marriage with someone you no longer love? How soon after you begin dating do you think you'd have sex?"

I silently gasped in horror! Was I actually hearing what I thought? I was so stunned I could not even comment on or question what this man was asking. As I sat in his office with a metaphorical knife in my heart, I vaguely remember hearing them talk about my husbands upcoming sexual adventures. This licensed professional (and I use that term very loosely) made disturbing recommendations which my husband seemed in agreement with. My suspicions that this counselor was biased were confirmed when my therapist regrettably informed me he was, at that time, going through his own divorce. He brought his personal life into our session. How could my husband or I determine if the advice he was giving was in our best interest? Clearly he had his own agenda and was presently incapable of offering impartial guidance to us.

My point is this - each of us is flawed in our thinking due, in part, to our past experiences and unresolved issues. If I had a terrifying incident with a dog when I was young, perhaps I was chased or bitten, how can I provide sound direction for my friend who inquires if she should get a canine for her children? Hard as I try to be objective, there is a residual fear eclipsing my impartiality. I may tell my friend of my prior experience and create a litany of reasons why buying a pooch for children is a bad idea. I can further my case by providing statistics on the number of children who are bitten, mauled or killed by dog attacks each year. And while I'm at it, I can toss in information about allergies and germs, shedding, and vet bills. Ugh! I can project my fear onto her, thus tainting her ability to make an objective determination. While my motives may be of sincere concern for the safety and well-being of her family, can she completely trust my counsel? Should she choose to not purchase a dog, is that really what is best? What about the benefits of teaching children responsibility or the lessons in unconditional love? Am I, as her advisor, absolutely certain I have guided her in the right direction? There is no way for me to be 100% sure. The mother, trusting in my judgment (after all, I do make some valid points) follows my lead and denies her children the privilege of owning Fido. But can she ever be confident her decision was the right one? After all, I am only human and do not have all the correct answers.

In-Decisions

Some of you may be thinking, "Janet, this is no big deal. If the kids want a dog they can get one when they grow up." And I agree – they can. This is not an issue of life-or-death but is meant to illustrate a point - in seeking the answers to life's questions, how can we ever be certain we are making the right choice?

You get my point – it's hard. Should I go to college right after high school or backpack through Europe for a year? My boyfriend just dumped me. Should I tell his new girlfriend what a jerk he is or let her find out on her own? Do I have plastic surgery to take years off my face or convince myself crow's feet add character? (They do, by the way.)

Like each of us, I strive to make good decisions. I take into consideration the pros and cons of each situation. What most impressed me about my time in philosophy class was the necessity and significance of examining each perspective and all options. I've trained myself to think beyond the moment, to ask thought provoking questions such as, "If I do ___, then ___may happen." Is that what I'm seeking? Will this benefit me now and in the future? Is this my best option? And what about those around me - how will my decision impact them? Will it help or hurt them now and in the future?

There are times that I literally agonize over choosing from the options before me. I have procrastinated and prolonged the inevitable. It's rare that I am ever 100% certain or comfortable with my choices. I care deeply about those in my close circle of family and friends. I also care about my community, my colleagues, and even strangers. I am concerned about our planet and all who inhabit it, including plant and animal life, our oceans, and streams - even insects. (Well, maybe not all insects - not mosquitoes and ticks and stink bugs, that's for sure.) Yet they are an important part of our eco-system and need to be respected as such (as long as they stay away from me).

Nine (Count 'Em!)Coats of Paint

I venture to say I am not alone in this challenge. I know many other conscientious individuals who are fearful of wrong choices. Perhaps for some this stems from low self-esteem. To fail or make a mistake can be humiliating and painful. The judgments and opinions of others play an important role in our lives. Criticisms are a difficult pill to swallow and can further damage a fragile ego. Procrastination becomes a form of self-preservation. "It is better to remain uncommitted than to embarrass myself by making the wrong choice."

Fear of facing the consequences of a bad decision can also lead to indecisiveness. "What if this ruins my life and I live to regret it?" Apprehension can be debilitating and leave some stuck in mediocrity. "Best if I stay put. At least I can't make matters worse." However, this mindset can easily lead to regret. Time passes and the *what if's* begin to surface. "What if I had taken that job overseas? Maybe I would be happier than I am now." "What if I had lost that weight, saved more money, gone to college, gotten married, stayed single…."

A lost opportunity may never reappear and we are left to live in doubt and regret.

"Maybe I could have been more…" You'll never know for sure.

The decision making process can be quite complex - so many questions and no guarantees. Will this decision benefit me? Will I still feel the same a week from now, six months from now or in ten years? What about my family - how will this affect them and others? What about future generations or the world in general? Maybe I'm over thinking. Maybe I should just throw caution to the wind and do what feels good at that moment. I know plenty of people who live that way and their lives seem none the worse for it. Heck, I've known people who have gotten lost following the directions of an expensive GPS and others who fly by the seat of their pants and have amazing adventures.

I need to trust myself more. So what if I make a mistake or something doesn't turn out exactly the way I planned? Hopefully, I can fix it and if not I'll make the best of it. Several years ago I painted my living and dining room *nine times* before settling on the right color. (True story, I promise.) You'd think I would have painted a test area first to see if I liked the shade but no - I was so confident I had made the perfect selection, I proceeded to paint two entire rooms top to bottom. When the paint dried I discovered, to my dismay, it was not at all what I wanted. (My husband just watched in silent disbelief.) I wasted a lot of time, energy, and money. But no one died. *Not a big deal*, I told myself. It's become somewhat of a family joke - one that will undoubtedly be handed down for generations to come. At least I've given my family something to laugh about.

The (Most) High Way

Getting back to Mr. Sinatra's signature song - further lyrics illustrate he's lived a full life and "did it my way". (*His* way, not *mine* – I just wanted to clear that up should there be any confusion. I didn't even know Mr. Sinatra.) That singular refrain repeats itself throughout the song.

I cannot count the number of artists who have recorded "My Way" and how many others are moved by its significance. Dare I be politically incorrect to say I find it to be somewhat self-serving? I do believe it was meant to portray the courage of one willing to take life by the horns, to face adversity and uncertainty with conviction, and proceed in a way both fulfilling and satisfying to him. And I give credit to those who live fearlessly. But did the lyricist take into account how a *my way* life impacts the lives of others? Was the well-being of those affected by the singer's decisions even considered?

Mr. Sinatra continues by stating he speaks what he truly feels but is it at the expense of the other party? Does he take into consideration how the other person may feel? Is he being rude? Would saying nothing at all and possibly sparing their feelings be better? Boasting of not being "one who kneels", in my mind, is arrogant and indicates one who lacks grace and compassion.

Keep in mind - this is all speculation on my part. I am not privy to the intention behind the music, although I can say with some degree of certainty there are those who have interpreted the lyrics as I've expressed and aligned their lives with a *my way* mentality.

I would be remiss if I did not address the final stanza as well. To paraphrase - if a man does not have himself, he has nothing. *Himself?* What about God? What role, if any, does our Creator play in his life? A life lived in ego (*me* oriented) is shallow and self-serving. One centered on God's way is fulfilling and genuine. "If not his *Lord*, then he has naught." That's better.

We have become such a self-absorbed society. We live in the moment, do what we want and say what we feel. And while all of this is well and good, it can cause extensive damage to those experiencing the fallout of *my way* living. I tried for many years to live my life according to what I wanted and made a huge mess of things. Perhaps it's time to try something new - *"Lord, show me how to live life, now, I'll do it God's way."*

CHAPTER 2

Ah-Ha Moments

In his book, <u>Self Matters</u>, Dr. Phil McGraw, bestselling author and TV host, says we all have ten defining moments, seven critical choices, and five pivotal people in our lives who define who we are and/or redirect the course of our lives. While I've never actually counted mine, I know for certain there are at least three significant moments that redefined me and dramatically altered the way in which I live my life.

Defining Moment 1

My first defining moment is easily recalled with crystal clarity - it began with the unexpected termination of my thirteen-year marriage. Without warning, my high school sweetheart announced he no longer wanted me as his wife, citing only that we had *drifted apart*. (Drifted apart? Really? After eighteen years together, that's all he's got?) The year was 1982. I had been a stay-at-home mom for twelve years and had just re-enrolled in college to complete my degree in psychology. The prior year had been a challenging one including the diagnosis of my (then) nine-year-old son with glaucoma in his right eye. Surgery and treatment over the past year yielded discouraging results and additional surgeries in the immediate future were imminent. In total, he had seven surgeries in the following nine months, all without success.

Additionally, I was unexpectedly thrust back into the work-force to help support my young family. Due to the unpredictability of my son's treatments, I was unable to sustain a traditional job. I was hired and fired in a single day from what appeared to be promising employment. Desperate times call for desperate measures so I began a home-based business which I successfully ran for the next sixteen years. However, the stress of everything I was dealing with was more than I could bear (or so I thought at the time) and I subsequently developed an eating disorder as a coping mechanism. I was drowning in fear and pain. (The story I'm about to share is one reserved only for close friends and select family members so I ask that you keep this confidential, ok? Thanks. Oh, wait...)

About six weeks into our separation, I awoke one morning suffocating in despair. As I swung my legs over the side of my bed, I knew they would buckle should I attempt to stand. The additional weight of the hopelessness resting upon my shoulders was more than my five-foot, two-inch frame could support. Tears welled up in my eyes. "I can't do this", I cried out to God. "It's too much. I have nothing inside me."

Instantly, a gentle Presence filled the room. It permeated every inch from wall to wall, ceiling to floor. Strong, protective, and comforting – it was distinct from anything I had ever experienced. Presence was not of this world but of one outside the realm of human understanding. Most pronounced was the intense sensation of Love. Unlike the equivalent human experience, this was pure, sacred, holy, and unconditional. I knew instinctively I was in the presence of the Divine. I felt arms of reassurance envelop me as I felt Presence convey words without speaking. "Why are you so afraid? I am here and will never allow anything to happen to you."

Instantly, calmness infused every cell of my being, removing all anguish, and restoring my strength. I rose to my feet. Intention complete, Presence softly retreated, leaving hope and serenity in place of sorrow, which by now had dissipated into a harmless memory.

I had been in the Holy Presence of God and in an instant my life was forever changed. I knew with great certainty I could face and conquer whatever life put in my path for I had the unconditional and ever-present strength of God within and around me - from fear to faith in under sixty seconds.

A fleeting moment in the presence of our Lord changes one for all eternity.

I rarely share this story as words can not accurately convey the magnitude of what I experienced. As poignant as it sounds, my encounter with God far exceeds what I have written.

To say "God is Love" is akin to saying the Universe is big. Unless you have experienced the Father in perfect form, you cannot fully appreciate my narrative. When I was a child I loved my dog Chips and thought I knew what love was. At age fifteen, I met my future husband and declared, "Now I know love!" But then my first child was born

> "Eye has not seen, nor ear heard, neither have entered into the heart of man, the things which God has prepared for them that love Him." ~ 1 Corinthians 2:9

and I knew emphatically, "There is no love greater than this!" And now I can say with even greater certainty - if you think you know love now, you will be in awe when you stand before the face of God, for God's love is not of this world. That's all I can say.

Well, Janet, that's a lovely story. But how did that define your life?

God is Out of My Mind

Knowing God, *truly* knowing God - not in your head as most of us know Him but in your heart - transforms you. It's like knowing health. We all know being healthy means being free of disease, feeling strong, and being void of pain or physical restrictions. We know it in our head. But most people don't experience it in their bodies. Most have some physical ailments - allergies, back pain, headaches, diabetes or worse. We have days when we feel relatively strong and healthy - our arthritis isn't acting up or that wretched cancer momentarily rests in obscurity, providing false respite. But imagine for a moment, what it would feel like to *experience* perfect health? For anyone who has ever recovered from a serious illness, it is easy to compare the profound differences. Being completely *healed* from physical imperfections invites an entirely new understanding of health and transforms the way in which we live our lives. Every joy is magnified and every opportunity is appreciated. There is an undeniable change in our internal as well as external being. It radiates from every cell of our existence. It is reflected in every decision we make, every encounter we have with others, and every word spoken.

So it is with genuinely knowing God. God *is* Love. There is no distinction. They are one and the same.

To experience perfect Love, unconditional, without judgment or restriction creates a yearning for more.

Each day, I long to be at one with the source of perfect Love. I yearn to have Divine Love reflected in me and through me so that in everything I do, in everything I say, with everyone I encounter, I am Love manifest in form. (Just for the record, I haven't perfected this yet but I am making remarkable progress, so, hooray for me!)

Each morning, I remind myself of who I am as I recite the following prayer...

"Lord, I am a physical manifestation of your presence in this world. Let all who know me come to know you through me. Help me to live my life today and everyday in a way that pleases you. For you alone are my Lord, you alone are my God, you alone are my Savior. Amen."

Having felt the love of God in its unadulterated form, it is fundamentally important for me to bring that love to others in all I say and do.

Nothing in life matters more to me than this - to be a living example of the Father's love.

Defining Moment 2

Both my mother and I strive to lead deeply spiritual lives and prayer is an integral part of our daily routine. Long ago, I came to understand that prayer does not change things. We pray for *stuff* that many times fails to materialize. (*I'm still waiting for that pony, God, like the one my sister got. What's up with that?*) It's easy to become disenchanted with God until you understand prayer changes *people*, more specifically, the hearts and minds of the one who's praying.

Prayer changes the heart of the one who is praying.

You might pray for a diamond bracelet from your husband for your birthday. And while you may not receive it, prayer can help you appreciate the sterling silver bangle he gave you instead by infusing your heart with gratitude.

Whenever my mom or I uncover a new prayer we pass it along to each other. The following arrived in my mailbox one day:

PRAYER OF MOTHER THERESA   1/10/19

People are often unreasonable, illogical, and self-centered.
Forgive them anyway.
If you are kind people may accuse you of selfish, ulterior
    motives.
Be kind anyway.
If you are successful, you will win some false friends and
    some true enemies.
Succeed anyway.
If you are honest and frank people may cheat you.
Be honest and frank anyway.
What you spend years building someone could destroy
    overnight.
Build anyway.
If you find serenity and happiness they may be jealous.
Be happy anyway.
The good you do today people will often forget tomorrow.
Do good anyway.

*Give the world the best you've got and it may never be
   enough.
Give the world the best you've got anyway.
You see, in the final analysis it is between you and God.
It never was between you and them anyway.*

This is a lovely prayer, I thought. Every line is rich with substance. I examined each verse word-for-word, seeking ways in which I could apply it to my life.

Verse One - Forgiveness

"People are often unreasonable, illogical, and self-centered. Forgive them anyway."

People, not *me*, right? Mother Theresa was clearly speaking about everyone else otherwise she would have said *"You* are unreasonable..." because as we all know, it's the rest of the world that's selfish. (All those who have never been unreasonable or self-centered raise your hand. Just as I thought.)

Have you ever been called narrow-minded, stubborn or pig-headed? The *my-way-or-the-highway* attitude is a perfect example. When I was single, I dated a guy for a very short period of time (you'll understand why in a minute). He was great in so many ways - funny, kind, smart, and hard-working. But he had one major flaw. As young as he was, he was set in his ways. There was a particular way he did things and no one was going to change him. He had a routine that worked for him and whoever was going to date, or eventually marry, him needed to understand that. So predictable was he that he used to joke he would be an easy target for anyone who wanted to assassinate him. "I do the exact same thing in the exact same way at precisely the same time every day."

This behavior provided a sense of security for him. He left home when he was only sixteen (not by choice) and had to figure out life on his own. Having a routine made him feel somewhat in control. Change created anxiety as he felt his power being relinquished to another. It was fear that kept him imprisoned in his habits. That was not something I wanted to live with.

Even those who are passionate about what they are doing or what they want can be seen as unreasonable to those who differ in opinion. A mother making herself a priority over her children is labeled selfish when perhaps her motive is akin to what I call the *oxygen mask principle* - when onboard an airplane, in the event of an emergency, place the oxygen mask on yourself first. In that way, you are better equipped to assist others. Perhaps, she realizes she must first care for herself so she may more effectively tend to the needs of her family. Others may fail to recognize her motives.

Regardless, each of us has reasons (whether or not others are aware of what they are) that drive us to do the things we do. Unresolved personal issues cloud good judgment and restrict rational behavior. We all have them (the personal issues). Therefore, it is imperative not to judge others but to be compassionate towards them for their struggles, pain, insecurities, ignorance, and so forth, that drive their actions. After all, if I have not yet reached a state of perfection (at times, I'm so far off-course at I'm not even sure what state I'm in!) then how can I expect it of others?

> *"Forgive us our trespasses as we forgive those who have trespassed against us..."*
> *– the Lord's Prayer*

Forgiveness is not an event - it is a process.
It removes judgments and expectations,
alleviates anger and resentment, fosters

compassion and understanding, and allows for a spiritual and emotional healing. It is, in fact, the path to inner peace and serenity.

~

Some people believe that when you have your health you have everything. I believe that when you have inner peace you have all you'll ever need.

~

(For a deeper understanding of forgiveness, check out a powerful and inspirational message @ www. FromGodWithLove.net.)

Verse 2 - Kindness 1/10/19

"If you are kind, people may accuse you of selfish, ulterior motives. Be kind anyway."

I cannot recall a single incident in my life when I harbored ulterior motives for something I did. I said *recall* because I might be mistaken. I don't think I am but it's always a possibility. I am one of the kindness people you'll ever meet. (Stop by someday, you'll see. I'll bake some cookies – double chocolate chip – outrageously delicious!) My therapist, from years ago, once commented, "You can figure out a person's needs and fulfill them before the individual even realizes they need something!" No one's ever had to ask me twice. If there is anything I can do to make your life easier or better I will. *I try!*

There are some who have accused me of surreptitious intentions and that hurts. One such incident involved a family member. This particular person, I'll call him *Rodney*, was behind in his mortgage payments. He was in danger of losing his home. Selling was not an option and he had no where else to go. And besides, his house was filled with decades of fond memories he did not want to say goodbye to.

I've always been fond of Rodney - he's a good person. I was in a position where I was able to offer some financial assistance. I approached him and asked if he could use my help. "I'd be more than happy to lend you some money to bring you up to date on your payments. There's no rush to pay me back and no interest." Rodney seemed interested until (you guessed it) I asked him to sign an agreement. The contract consisted of four sentences written in simple English (no legal gobbledygook). Easy to understand, it stated the amount borrowed and for what purpose plus a simple clause stating the money was to be paid back upon request. (That was to ensure the loan would not exist ad infinitum. And should I suddenly find myself in need of its return, I wanted to ensure I could recall it.) I explained that, with the exception of an extreme emergency, I did not foresee that happening. All that was needed was his signature.

I was astonished and deeply hurt when Rodney lashed out at me. "You just want to get your hands on my house! If I can't pay you back, you're going to take it from me!" I was speechless! I couldn't even respond to his outrageous accusations nor could I fathom where they were coming from. "I'm not signing *anything*!" Rodney screamed! "You're trying to cheat me!"

Attempts to calm him down and reassure him, as well as prove my intentions, were futile. He was completely unreasonable. I was crushed. Never (and I do mean never) in my life have I done something for someone with thought of personal gain. It broke my heart.

I have met many people who've been burned - people who went out of their way to be kind or helpful to someone or to do something purely out of the goodness of their heart. They were often unappreciated, accused of not actually doing it, criticized for not doing it right or blamed because something went wrong after-the-fact. Filled with bitterness and resentment, they begrudgingly declared they would never again do something nice for anyone (or at least not for that particular person). Their disappointment and hurt robbed them of any future joy and turned their hearts to stone.

I knew Rodney had been cheated before and was skeptical and guarded. I would eventually overcome the hurt but I refused to allow this incident to sour me on kindness. To change who I am based on someone else's issues would only hurt me. It would create an internal conflict (*I want to be caring but I must hold back to protect myself*) that would lead to unhappiness and discontent within myself. I was not willing to make that sacrifice.

Never allow another person's bad behavior to change who you are.

I decided to honor God and continue to share with others the gift of generosity He blessed me with.

Verse 3 - Succeed

"If you are successful, you will win some false friends and some true enemies. Succeed anyway."

We've all heard of people who have achieved great success and suddenly everyone they've ever met crawls out of the woodwork proclaiming to be their best friend. For some, they are genuinely happy for the other's accomplishments and want to acknowledge them. But for others, they seek to reap personal gain from the connection.

Unknowns have married Hollywood celebrities for the sole purpose of cashing in on their fame. They become celebrities by proxy, sometimes being afforded acting roles in the world of stardom. Some marry the rich to avoid having to take responsibility for their own lives and support themselves financially. Some May/December romances may help recapture an aging individual's fading youth.

I've spent many years building a successful speaking career. Prior to this, I owned a small home repair business. While not a glamorous job, I did quite well financially, though never speaking publicly about that aspect of my company. Blue collar jobs are far from envious and many, like mine, do not require a PhD in spackling. I had plenty of friends, got along well with my family, and even my ex and I were on good terms. Periodically, some would inquire as to when I was going to get a *real* job. "You need to be doing more with your life." For now, as a single mother of four, this job suited my needs. In time, I would discover what my divine purpose was.

Things changed in the early ninety's when I was brought into the field of motivational speaking. This, I realized, was my passion and my new career took off like wild fire. Like any other business owner, I worked ridiculously long hours, skipped vacations, and reinvested most of my earnings back into my company. It wasn't long before I was speaking to Fortune 500 companies, giving seminar cruises for major cruise lines and getting paid extremely well to do so (hey, it's not all glamour – that salt air really brings out the frizz in my hair!). I became a sought after TV and radio personality and appeared word-wide in publications from Alaska to India. My books were doing well *and* my wardrobe significantly improved.

But success converted some allies into adversaries and those green with envy soon emerged. While I rarely speak about my career with anyone other than my mom and two of my closest friends, there were some who begrudged my accomplishments. I was accused of unprofessional and deceptive behaviors and my credentials were questioned. I was even accused of fabricating a list of prestigious clients. One person in particular, damaged my relationship with several prominent people in my life.

It is distressing to know others are envious of you. However, it is vitally important not to allow their insecurities to deter you from achieving what is important.

For those of you who are parents, does it make you happy to see your children discontented or sad? I'm hard pressed to find any mother or father who would respond affirmatively. We all want our children to be happy and when someone brings them down, we instruct them to ignore the other party. We want to shield them from disappointment and sadness and try our best to help restore their sense of joy.

When they do well in school - academically or in other areas - they are bound to be confronted with jealous schoolmates. Some will go so far as to criticize, belittle, bully, fight with or gossip about them. Once again, we rise to the occasion, teaching them that those who are jealous are insecure and don't feel good about themselves. "Be proud of who you are and your 4.0 GPA. You earned it. Don't worry about what others say. Your true friends will be happy with you."

In a recent entry in Dear Abby's daily advice column, a young man wrote of his parents who had retired and decided to travel the world. Years of frugal living enabled them to do so in the latter stage of their lives. The son was outraged and manipulative. He threatened to cut his parents out of his life if they didn't stop spending *his* inheritance. He was employing Abby's help in convincing them to save *his* money for him. She wisely reprimanded him and wished his parents a resounding *bon voyage*!

Be successful but enter into your relationships cautiously. When necessary, gently release those who are unsupportive, jealous or resentful.

Verse 4 - Honest and Candid   *1/17/19*

"If you are honest and frank people may cheat you. Be honest and frank anyway."

(Note - if you're not *Frank*, this does not apply. Get it? *Frank*? Never mind.)

Countless inventors have had their ideas stolen from them. Someone invents a creative new gadget designed to solve one of life's great problems and wham-o - before obtaining the patent it's being manufactured and sold by the very same guy who promised to help them develop and bring it to market.

I must admit that when I am writing a new book I may share the general concept with those who inquire but I never fully disclose the nature of what I am writing. Someone may *borrow* my idea and use it before I complete my project. While for the most part I believe people are honest, there is always the possibility an unsavory character is seeking to cash in on my knowledge and/ or name. I'm not willing to take that risk and therefore take the proper precautions to protect myself and my intellectual property. (The not-so-intellectual stuff is not worth stealing. Feel free to help yourself.)

There are those who encourage us to be truthful and candid with them. "Tell me what you really think of me." With wary trepidation, we openly share our thoughts. "You do look like you've put on a few pounds." "That dinner you prepared tasted like cardboard." "It's totally inappropriate of you to be flirting on the internet when you're married." The backlash of our requested honesty is sometimes met with anger, rage, and possibly a broken relationship. "How could you be so mean? I thought you were my friend." *But you just asked me to be honest,* you're thinking. *Jeeze Louise! I can't win! Next time, I'm just going to keep my mouth shut!*

Yet to remain silent when asked for a truthful response is cowardly. And to avoid a potential confrontation or the possibility of offending another for a known wrongdoing condones the bad behavior. Truth (different from opinion or perception) must prevail and can be achieved with the utmost dignity and sensitivity. "A lot of people gain weight. Your health is the most important thing. If you're not happy with the way you look or feel, I'm sure you'll do something about it."

Verse 5 - Build

"What you spend years building someone could destroy overnight. Build anyway."

At first reading, I am reminded of the World Trade Center. Recently our country celebrated the tenth anniversary of the terrorist destruction of the tallest buildings the world had ever seen and the senseless massacre of over 3,000 innocent lives. Yet even that was not enough to defeat the American spirit. Ours is a strong and proud nation and we have been through many battles, economic depressions, product shortages, and natural disasters. No one and nothing has yet been able to extinguish our fortitude and courage. Our resilience rises above the ashes to rebuild what we value.

In our personal lives as well, we do best when employing that same mental attitude and approach. One of my heroes is Carrie Lightner, mother and founder of

Mothers Against Drunk Driving. Ms. Lightner lost one of her twin daughters to a drunk driver but rather than allow the loss to derail her life, she set out on a passionate quest - to pass legislation making it a crime to drive while under the influence of alcohol. She took her pain and rechanneled it into purpose – protecting those at risk for serious injury or death due to intoxicated drivers. In spite of her tragic loss, she works tirelessly to remove dangerous drivers from our roadways. *Juan's Law*

The day my first husband ended our marriage, I made three promises to myself, my children and God. One such promise was - if I was unable to save my marriage and was in possession of divorce papers with a judge's signature on them, I would take my current situation and rebuild a new and better life for myself. Somewhat taken aback by this unfamiliar attitude, I was equally energized by the unlimited possibilities that lay before me. I was determined not to be defeated - neither emotionally, spiritually nor financially - by a selfish twist of fate.

Forgiveness and Benadryl

My ex-husband and I had an amicable relationship during and for many years after our divorce. As long as I was poor, alone, and struggling, things were fine between us. But upon discovering I was a very successful business woman and also had a special man in my life, he became jealous and vindictive. Rivaling the National Inquirer, vicious lies and rumors began circulating causing immeasurable damage in my most intimate family relationships. This, in part, contributed to a long estrangement from my children. While there was a deep sadness in my heart for what was occurring, nothing could ever serve as a deterrent to fulfilling my mission in life. Jealousy and mosquitoes have been around since the creation of man. That's why God gave us forgiveness and Benadryl.

God does not want us to live in fear, to be ruled by the dictates and issues of others. One of my favorite passages from the Bible is found in Jeremiah:

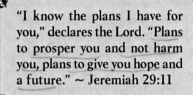

> "I know the plans I have for you," declares the Lord. "Plans to prosper you and not harm you, plans to give you hope and a future." ~ Jeremiah 29:11

Keep building.

Verse 6 - Happiness

"If you find serenity and happiness they may be jealous. Be happy anyway."

Ah, the naysayers, pessimists, and dream-slayers - they're all around us, ready to pounce on our joy at every opportunity. They seem to posses a compulsion to make the rest of the world as miserable as they are. They are allergic to smiles, believe laughter causes cavities, cheerfulness can lead to osteoporosis, and serenity makes hair grow out of strange places on our bodies. Statements such as "What are *you* so happy about?" and "Life stinks!" frequently emanate from their vocal orifices. On one occasion, I actually had someone sarcastically comment to me, "No one can be that happy and positive all the time!" (They were referring to me.) My reply was simply, "OK." I don't argue with cynics.

I've worked hard at being peaceful. (Does that sound as odd reading it as it does writing it? It reeks of oxymoron-ism.) What I mean is - I haven't always been a person of serenity. Happiness was always temporarily out of stock whenever I placed an order. I believed that I was not meant to be happy. Fleeting moments of delight might perch upon my shoulder only to be promptly shattered by life's harsh realities. My life consisted of single handedly pushing giant boulders up mountainous terrain…in the snow…barefoot…with my little brother on my back. Everything was a relentless struggle. People were constantly raining on my parade and sabotaging any moment of peace or joy I had discovered.

Somewhere in my forties (not the 1940's - I was barely born then!) I decided I had had enough misery. I realized I couldn't stop bad things from happening and I couldn't fix other people's misery. But I made a conscious decision I was going to be cheerful *no matter what*. I was going to smile and sing (well, I always sing - all day, every day). But rather than seek happiness, I decided to pursue gratitude*. I chose to look at everything in my life - all the blessings, the losses, the good, the bad, and the ugly - as reason to give thanks. Rather than be miserable because my best friend moved away, I felt deeply grateful for the years we were neighbors. I also gave thanks for the technology that keeps us connected. *reframing experience*

When a freak storm dropped twelve inches of rain on our home in less than twenty-four hours and flooded our basement, my husband and I spend spent fourteen consecutive hours siphoning water up off our basement floor. He cursed and complained non-stop. I found a yellow rubber duck (one of my seminars props – email me, I'll explain) and floated it upon the water. I sang songs from Sesame Street ("Rubber ducky you're the one…") while simultaneously vacuuming up H2O. I looked stunning in my second-hand, thigh-high, sunflower yellow fireman boots, for which I was eternally grateful. (I hate having wet feet!) The surprising result of gratitude is, ironically, joy.

---

*   (Read The Happiness Hype @ http://www.pfeiffer powerseminars.com/pps1-newsletter.html#hype)

I also discovered the path to inner peace. (Wayne Dyer says that there is no way to peace. Peace *is* the way. Brilliant!) Peacefulness is as simple as removing all expectations and allowing life to unfold naturally. Anger is actually the direct result of unmet expectations. (Read The Secret Side of Anger by yours truly.) We have so many idealistic and impractical expectations of others, ourselves, God, and the world in general. When our demands are not forthcoming, we become frustrated, disappointed, and angry. Like a toddler throwing a tantrum when things don't go their way, our behavior is simply larger in scale. "Hold on a second, Janet. You're talking apples and oranges. A child throwing a hissy fit because he can't fit his Lego pieces together is not nearly as serious as someone whose car breaks down on the way to the most important job interview of his career." Well, I beg to differ. Just ask the child. It matters as much to him as the other does to the adult. It's all a matter of perception. In hindsight, missing that interview might be a blessing in disguise. It's reminiscent of the businessman who missed his bus and never made it to work at the World Trade Center on Sept. 11, 2011.

So much of what we place importance on in reality has little, if any, real significance. Ideally, the older and wiser we get, the more evident this truth becomes. Yet for many, it is difficult, if not impossible, to believe there are those of us who truly are at peace with ourselves and our circumstances. (Being *at peace with*, by the way, is not synonymous with *being happy about*. I learned to be at peace with the ten years I was estranged from my children. I was never happy about it.)

My faith in God allows me to be at peace with that which I have no control over - all things external.

As I sit at my computer, I glance down at my feet. There are two of my newest canine babies, Willow and Butterscotch, curled up and sound asleep in their beds. No cares. No worries. Just eat, sleep, play, and pee. That's it. That's the formula for happiness and inner peace. They put no expectations or demands on one another or on me for that matter. They are blessed with the wisdom to allow life to unfold naturally and not concern themselves with trivial matters, like who's wearing the newer leash (Butterscotch) or who's smarter (Willow). They care only about being content and happy. Willow's snoring is a clear indication of her level of contentment.

A Dam Problem

Ever notice how a stream flows effortlessly through the landscape? It doesn't labor to find its way to the ocean. It chooses the path of least resistance, concerned only in reaching its assigned destination. When confronted with an obstruction, it does not complain or fight. It simply redirects its flow to one more accessible - no effort. Leave it to man to construct a dam and interrupt its natural course. Water strains against the unnatural blockage, causing damage. Man must continually work to repair the dam, expending precious energy which could have been more wisely assigned to other tasks. What sense is there in that?

When I finally learned to remove all comparisons, judgments, and expectations of others, the result was inner peace and serenity. I work diligently but without force. Whatever happens, I accept as an unexpected opportunity to learn and grow, while anticipating the blessings yet to come.

Do not concern yourself with the naysayers and pessimists. Jealousy is their issue. Be happy and grateful regardless. It's your life.

Verse 7 - Do Good

"The good you do today people will often forget tomorrow. Do good anyway."

What is the alternative - to do poorly or to not do at all? How does that improve your life or the lives of those around you? Clearly it doesn't yet many fall prey to that mindset.

"I'm tired of working hard at my job and never getting any recognition!" "I've sacrificed everything for my children and they're so ungrateful!" "I volunteered at the hospital for ten years and no one even gave me so much as a card when I retired. That's the last time I do anything nice for anybody!"

Too often we feel we are the only ones who perform good deeds that go unnoticed and fall into the snare of self-pity (which happens to be the highway to misery). There are millions of people around the globe who work hard and are never appreciated. In fact, I'll venture to say that the efforts of the vast majority fall below the radar. Imagine what the world would look like if suddenly they all ceased doing good? Imagine how many lives would suffer by not having Little League coaches, Girl Scout leaders, EMT's, and volunteer fire fighters, not to mention those who work so tirelessly to raise funds for the less fortunate? Imagine all the elderly who would be left to fend for themselves because family members and friends were offended they weren't honored for their selfless efforts?

What is the reason we work hard at our jobs, spend years sacrificing for our children or forgo vacations to assist strangers rebuild their homes after a hurricane? Do we labor for the glory, praise, fame or perhaps monetary gain of such endeavors? If so, then our efforts stem from ego and are selfish in nature.

Or, do we do what we do because we feel in our hearts it's the right thing? Are we motivated by the pleasure and satisfaction we receive from a job well done? Do we take personal delight in seeing the end result of our hard work and sacrifice? If that is the case, then to cease doing so would cause great sadness in us. By denying our own pleasure, we ultimately punish ourselves.

In essence, we cut off our nose to spite our face and it's pretty darn hard to breathe without a nose! Think about it - a nose serves many valuable purposes. It allows us to breathe in much needed oxygen in order to sustain our lives. It filters out harmful bacteria that might otherwise infiltrate our lungs should we inhale through our mouths. It warms, cleans, and humidifies the air we breathe, and keeps our respiratory tract clean and moist. It supports our glasses so we can enjoy better vision. And it's a lovely appendage on which to display jewelry. (Ok, maybe not the latter so much.)

Doing good also serves some very important functions in our daily lives - it connects us to one another, allows us to express the God within, brings us feelings of pleasure, boosts self-esteem and confidence, enhances our relationships, and more. There is also evidence it boosts our immune system, thereby resulting in an overall improvement in health.

This past summer, I ventured out on a lofty goal - I was determined to raise $10,000 for Sacred Heart Church in Camden, N.J. Camden is the second poorest city in the US as well as the second most violent. If I found ten churches willing to host a lecture/book signing and each church got one hundred people to attend, I could easily reach my goal. With absolutely no cost or effort on the church's part, it seemed like a slam-dunk.

So I began marketing my event by sending out emails detailing the great need in Camden and my strategy for raising money. *Surely*, I thought, *I'll get a huge response.* Not so. After spending four months promoting it, I found two churches willing to help. Both pastors are personal friends of mine. I was disheartened to say the least. The event was very inexpensive to attend - people got a great lecture focusing on creating inner peace *and* a free copy of <u>The Secret Side of Anger</u>. Who could say "No" to that? Nearly three hundred churches, that's who.

Discouraged, I proceeded anyway. After all, some effort will produce some success, which is better than none. If I can only raise twenty dollars, to a mother who cannot afford diapers for her baby, that's a lot of money. I gave my first lecture at St. Patrick's Church in nearby Chatham. We had a nice group of people who were delightful to speak to. As they entered the lecture hall with their payment, many handed me more money than was requested. When I reached to give them change, I was told to keep the extra - it was for a good cause. Several people were unable to attend and sent in very generous donations. I was blown away! That evening, I raised considerably more than anticipated.

The following day, I received another email from a parish wanting to sign up to host an event. *Wonderful*, I thought! *That makes three. It's getting better.* As I sit here typing, my phone interrupts me with yet another church requesting the same. Imagine if had I given up simply because no one was cooperating with me? What initially seemed to be an epidemic of apathy actually turned out to be a case of <u>delayed respon</u>se.

Severing our proboscis from our face would certainly detract from our physical beauty as well as inhibit our ability to fully inhale life. Ceasing to perform good deeds causes ugliness (aka selfishness) and severely hampers our full enjoyment of life on many levels. Do not concern yourself with those who have deficient memories. Do good anyway.

Verse 8 - Give and Give

"Give the world the best you've got and it may never be enough. Give the world the best you've got anyway."

It amazes me how this world continues to spin on its axis and hasn't yet tipped over from the uneven distribution of generosity (and I'm not simply referring to that of a monetary nature). There is a terrible imbalance between those who give and those who don't, and worse - those who continually take. We've all experienced frustration over the distribution of government assistance in this country - there are some who manipulate the system and drain the American taxpayers of their financial resources. And consider the charitable organizations whose noble causes pulls at our heartstrings - we donate only to learn the money earmarked to assist those in need actually fell into the pockets of the administrators.

Several years ago, a plea for much needed financial assistance due to a recent natural disaster prompted me to make a substantial donation to one of the largest non-profits in the world - one I believed to be reputable. Later it was brought to my attention that the head of this organization earns nearly half a million dollars annually. Needless to say, I was deeply distressed and saddened by what I believed to be a deceitful practice. Deciding to never again contribute to this particular association, I chose not to allow it to sour me on donating in general. It did, however, teach me to do my homework and carefully research any 501C3's before swiping my credit card again.

Children grow up in homes with parents who are never satisfied with who they are and what they accomplish. I remember in particular a young boy name "Joe". He and my son were seven years old at the time and played PAL baseball on the same team. Even at such a tender age, Joe was clearly a natural. Whether pitching or batting, he far surpassed other players in the league.

He was known for the many home runs he scored as well as pitching no-hitters. Yet no matter how hard he tried, and no matter how much he excelled, he was never good enough for his father. From the bleachers, you could hear his father screaming at him to do better: "Throw harder!" "Pitch harder!" "Run faster!" Although Joe could easily bring his team to victory each week, he himself could never win. The criticism took its toll. By age twelve, Joe's cleats were put out at a family garage sale.

My bi-monthly anger management support group is filled with people from every walk of life. One gentleman attended faithfully for several months. With three other siblings, he was the only one willing to accept the responsibility of his elderly parents. Moving them into his tiny home, he shouldered not only the physical demands of caring for their ever-increasing needs but most of the financial burden. On occasion, he would reach out to his sisters for a much needed reprieve. "Just a few hours on a Sunday afternoon, that's all I ask for. They groan and complain that they don't have the time." No matter how much he gave, they expected more. In their minds, because he had taken on the responsibility it alleviated them of theirs.

These past few years have presented enormous challenges for American businesses. Thousands of workers have been laid off leaving behind employees who are expected to pick up the slack. My husband is one such worker. Two years ago, his company cut workers hours by five per week yet the men were expected to complete the same forty hours of work in thirty-five. Two men were also laid off which added an additional burden to their workload. None were compensated for the additional stress and efforts. Each night, my husband returned home discouraged and disheartened. The morale of the company was in the gutter. Each day, those remaining cared less and less. When I asked my husband why he didn't just do the bare minimum and not give a rat's patooty about the quality of his work (after all, his boss doesn't care about him), I was not the least bit surprised by his response. "I can't", he stated. "This is about my customers who depend on me to do a good job. And besides, I need to feel good about myself at the end of the day." Ah, integrity - he does good because it matters to him, accolades or not.

Too often, we allow the ungratefulness of others to embitter us and we deny our virtuous nature. In essence, we allow others to change who we are. *don't give others the power over you*

> *When our outward actions are not*
> *congruent with our intrinsic nature,*
> *we create internal conflict and misery.*

Do good. It matters.

Verse 9 - A Spotlight Moment 2/7/19

Then I read the final two lines and my life was forever changed.

> **"You see, in the final analysis it is between**
> **you and God. It never was between you and**
> **them anyway."**

Holy moly! Me and God! *My life has nothing at all to do with others - it has everything to do with me and God!*

> *My life is exclusively about my relationship*
> *with God.*

The critical mistake almost all of us make is we erroneously believe our lives are about our children, spouses, parents, friends, bosses, coworkers, neighbors, strangers or jobs. Some mistakenly decide their lives are

As the Master desires

primarily about themselves. You know who I'm speaking about – those who believe the world revolves around them or those with a sense of entitlement - *the world owes me* attitude. (Sound like anyone you know? Be honest.) Life has absolutely not a single thing to do with any of that. It doesn't even have anything to do with *me*, per se. It is not about Janet the wife or mother or daughter, or Janet the author and inspirational speaker, or Janet the successful entrepreneur. It is not about needing to look a certain way or acquire degrees or recognition nor is it who Janet wants in her life or where she wants to live. And it for certain is *not* about any of *you*. (Hold on - before you call my mother and complain that her middle child just offended you and is an idiot, hear me out.)

Milkbone Pantsuits and Grape Juice

In today's world, there is a competitive methodology to the way most of us live. It's an *us vs. them* mentality. Some compete on a material or financial level. But for others there is the need to be right, to look younger, to be thinner, to have the higher level of education or more prestigious job or to date or marry someone *hot*. There's a need to be the favorite parent (or child), to gain recognition for our accomplishments and blame others for what went wrong, to seek justice for those who have offended us or committed a crime, or to have what we want and get what we deserve. It's a dog-eat-dog world and I'm wearing a Milkbone pantsuit. Come on - admit it. We have all lived our lives in this manner to some extent. I know I certainly have at times. Even those who are generous very often live ego-centered lives. We do what feels good or gets us what we're seeking.

We compete against coworkers to win the coveted promotion and corner office with the view. Athletes vie for the gold medal and product endorsements that precede a celebrity lifestyle. Divorcing spouses squander their life savings fighting over who gains custody of the eight-year-old microwave. Friends argue over who's fault it is that they were late for the movie premier. Parents brag about their protégé child performing on Broadway. And drivers battle it out on our highways at sixty-five miles per hour determined to prevent the other from cutting in front of them. Really, folks? The Hatfield's vs. McCoy's mentality is so counter-productive. Who even cares about this stuff? (Obviously someone cares or they wouldn't engage in such competitive, nonsensical, and adolescent behaviors.)

Remember when you were seven? You're little brother spilled grape juice all over his bed. Mom was furious! She came into the bedroom you both shared and began screaming, "For cryin' out loud! How many times have I told you *not* to drink juice in bed! Look at the mess you've made – your bed is ruined!" As your sibling burst into tears, you innocently looked up at your mother with the biggest brown eyes you could muster and sweetly declared, "I drank my juice in the kitchen like you said, Mom," head nodding affirmatively while seeking to remind her who her *good* child was. There wasn't even the slightest consideration of how your little brother was feeling as you extolled your own virtues. But he was six and you were seven - time to grow up and stop fighting to be right or to be loved more or to be better than.

In every scenario in our lives, God observes our response. Will we succumb to our human insecurities and allow others to separate us from the Divine? Will we relinquish Spirit to another's immaturities? Do we expend energy seeking what is fair rather than pursue our journey towards knowing God? When our focus is on how others perceive us or who has more or is more *right*, we sever our oneness with the Divine.

Mr. Right and Mommy Dearest

Is there someone in your life who always has to be right? This is an annoying trait that could drive even Mother Theresa herself to swear. (Just kidding, I think.) For most, we become incensed at the arrogance and pomposity of the other party. Determined not to let them *win* while believing it is our responsibility to put them in their place, we invest significant time and energy into proving them wrong. Failing to take into consideration they may suffer with a poor self-image, we forgo a compassionate response and put forth a valiant effort to embarrass or humiliate them.

My divorce was three decades ago. Even though he chose to end the marriage, I made a decision the split would be an amicable one. My attorney asked what I wanted from the marital home and in the form of spousal support. I asked for only what I was entitled to under the law. I would not drag him through the mire and make him pay for what he had done. Whatever the law deemed fair, regardless of my personal feelings, I would accept.

I made another important decision as well - to never put my children in the middle of our issues. I had no desire to be the favorite parent or the one viewed as the victim. There was love enough in their hearts for both of us and I had no intention of ever interfering with that natural affection. To this day, I have held true to that promise.

In my two decades as a motivational speaker and spiritual life coach as well as in my personal life, one matter that consistently presents itself is the issue between custodial and non-custodial parents. Couples choose to part ways after bringing a new life into this world. Animosity builds and the child becomes a pawn as custody, visitation, and child support become bones-of-contention. The child, caught in the middle, is denied a loving relationship with both parents as each punish and seek revenge for the most inane reasons. In extreme cases, this can lead to parental alienation. Not only have I endured what I believe was my own case but I have also assisted many clients struggling just to have some contact with their children. While focusing on hurting and controlling the other parent, the children are caught in the cross-fire and become innocent fatalities of jealousy and hate.

This behavior is based on the competitive need to be the good parent, the one who is right - the favorite. It has nothing at all to do with the needs, rights, and well-being of the children both claim to love beyond measure. It is purely ego, pride, selfishness, and greed.

God commands us to "Love one another as I have loved you" - completely, unconditionally, and without reservation. But in a situation such as divorce, how can one love the other who has betrayed them on such an intimate level? It is impossible when approached from a competitive ego-driven perspective - me vs. him. But from a spiritual standpoint (he/she is a beloved child of God as am I), it becomes effortless.

Once again, this situation is not meant to be a battle to prove who is the evil, bad, selfish or immoral parent. If it were, then the backstabbing, fighting, name calling, and court battles would be deemed acceptable and perhaps even necessary. However, if one subscribes to the belief revealed in the final stanza of Mother Theresa's prayer - that the entirety of our lives has nothing at all do to with the other party but instead is an opportunity between us and Creator to connect on a deeper more intimate level - then how we respond is based on His command and expectations, not on the other party's behavior or, for that matter, civil law's entitlement clause.

I can view confrontational people, judgmental statements, betrayals, favoritism, and such from a

whole scheme of things - between God & yourself

completely different perspective. I no longer need to be right, to have the last word or to win the approval of my family, friends, colleagues or society. Nor must I be more or achieve more in order to feel good about myself. All of that is irrelevant. I need only to concern myself with pleasing my Creator.

I applied this newfound philosophy to the first marathon I entered. My goal was simply to prove to myself I was competent enough to cross the finish line. And I did. I was oblivious to the other 300 plus race-walkers participating in the Fort Monmouth event in Sept of 1994. My focus was exclusively on crossing the finish line and completing the twenty-six mile course. Four hours and forty-three minutes later, I achieved what I had set out to. I attended the award ceremony with admiration for those who were awarded medals and satisfaction for my personal accomplishments (which, ironically, included three medals of my own).

Don't misunderstand - I do admire those with a competitive spirit and believe that in many instances it can be highly advantageous. A spirited edge pushes individuals to achieve higher goals in life. However, this attitude can prove counter-productive when the focus becomes proving to others you are superior to them.

Everything you experience, every person you encounter, every loss you endure is a personal moment between you and God.

Remove ego from the equation. He can only work through you when you forgo your own immature impulses and selfish desires. Turn to Him for guidance and follow His instruction.

His way deflects suffering and bestows blessings on all parties.

Consider the husband who puts his heart and soul into his marriage only to discover his wife is having an affair or an inventor who spends thousands of dollars and years of research and development on a new product only to have his idea stolen before getting it patented. There are thousands of authors who spend their life working on a great manuscript only to receive rejection after rejection from publishers. There's the child who studies tirelessly with aspirations of a college education only to discover his parents have squandered the money for his tuition. And what about the trusting young woman who dates a long-time friend only to be date raped?

Our hurt and outrage over such transgressions can easily lead to revenge, fear, bitterness, hatred, low self-esteem, pessimism, depression, apathy, and more. "You betrayed me!" "You hurt my feelings!" "You stole my idea. You had no right!" "I'll never forgive you for what you did." "I can never trust anyone ever again because of you." "You ruined my life!"

We spend precious time seeking justice but justice does not engender healing. One does not recover from an incident because the other party was punished. We still feel wronged and often carry the residual scars of inequity internally for the remainder of our lives.

Heads it's Love, Tails - a Jerk   2/28/19

Take a moment and do this exercise. It will help clarify what I mean. Visualize, if you will, walking along a beach with the love of your life. Arms wrapped tightly around one another, you share sentimental words of passion as you delight in the warmth of mutual affection. Suddenly, your romantic bliss is disrupted. An arrogant bully approaches and calls your sweetheart a derogatory name. You feel compelled to defend her/his reputation and put this guy in his place. You release your embrace from your beloved, pump yourself up in an intimidating posture, and challenge the jerk. A few choice words are exchanged as you prepare to take it to the next level, if necessary. Thankfully, he backs off and walks away. No harm done - or so it seems. But at the very moment you took personal offense to his behavior and assumed a defensive position, you disconnected from your love. Amorous feelings were interrupted and replaced with pride as your blissful encounter was temporarily suspended. You shifted gears and relinquished all feelings of oneness in order to address an external negative force with like feelings and behaviors. This response is purely ego based. *You can lose yourself to other's problems*

One forfeits love when consumed with anger and pride.

Now imagine, if you will, another option - the same scenario but with a different objective. Your feelings of amore are so intense you decide you are unwilling to surrender them. Choosing to remain emotionally detached from his behavior, you ignore him and continue walking along the beach. The further you remove yourself from the negative, the less it affects you as you remain as one with love. Bingo! We have a winner! Well, somewhat. While this is certainly a more mature reaction, there is yet an even more enlightened alternative - the *response* of love. You opt to address the individual without disconnecting from passion. In fact, love becomes the method of response. At the outset, love removes all judgments and labels as you recognize this person as one of God's precious children, your brother in Christ - not an idiot or jerk. He is a sacred creation of our Lord who is struggling with a personal demon. Your new awareness dictates a thoughtful response.

*The words and gestures which emanate
from your heart are tempered with
compassion.*

You maintain your serenity as you reply with a smile, "Have a blessed evening, sir." You have shared love, God's healing Love, with another human being. You have shown him God's Way and planted a seed for spiritual growth within him. There is no greater gift.

The Battle of Stupid

Many years ago, when I was much younger and infected with a moderate case of undiagnosed ego, I was driving along Hamburg Turnpike in Wayne, N.J. Becoming increasingly more frustrated at the shear number of drivers on the road, I found myself growing impatient. Didn't they realize I was on a tight schedule and didn't have time to waste being stuck in traffic? "Oh come on!" I shouted. "This is ridiculous! I have no time for people who don't know how to drive. Just get off the road for crying out loud!" This went on for several minutes (me vs. them in a mental battle of stupidity) when I finally discontinued my rant. "And that was 'Up on the Roof' by the Drifters", Cousin Brucie of 101.1 CBS FM proclaimed. What? I just missed one of my all-time favorite songs *ever* in the history of Oldies but Goodies because I was so wrapped up in my ridiculous self-righteous demands! I knew it could be *forever* before I heard that song again on the radio. I undoubtedly emerged victorious in the Battle of Stupid that day.

This may seem like an insignificant incident but it is meant to serve as an example of how easy it is to make our lives a battleground between us and them. Had I chosen to be more realistic and understanding of the needs and rights of others (Spirit) I could have spent those three minutes thoroughly enjoying a musical blast-from-the-past.

Grapefruits or God?

We forgo our own joy, serenity, happiness, and pleasure when we permit ego to gain control and dictate our behaviors. Furthermore, we run a significant risk of causing pain and suffering to others in the process. When we remain in Spirit, we reside in Love - pure, passionate, peaceful, harmonious bliss, and all around us benefit.

After nearly half a century on this planet, it was finally beginning to make sense. God wanted me to make the choices with my life that would not only be in my best interest but also aid others as well. (Doesn't being happy benefit me more than being sad as does forgiving rather than harboring grudges?) Was I willing to have absolute and abiding faith in Him, to have such deep and unqualified love that I was willing to completely obey His will without question or doubt? Was I willing to trust His judgment more than my own?

When I live my life according to the *Ten Commandments of Janet*, I sometimes make good decisions. Other times, not so much. Its hit and miss - sometimes I act intelligently, other times like a grapefruit. At times my choices yield a positive response but too often, I get hurt or, worse, cause suffering to others. I may think things are turning out a particular way and then all hell breaks loose. "Opps! Sorry. Not what I expected." But it's too late. The damage has been done and I and/or others are left to pick up the broken pieces of our lives and try to reassemble them, to make sense of what just happened, and to move forward. Subsequently, I live with the consequences and regret of what I have just

said or done. And regret, my friend, is a heavy burden
to carry.

— no do overs
— can apologize

God of Nike

As I was struggling through my decade of hell
in the 1980's and '90's, I felt as though I was being
tested. Was God allowing these trials to enter my life
to see if I would follow His Law? And was I also being
graded? If I failed would I get detention, or worse -
left back?

That image didn't conform to the God I know -
loving, kind, compassionate, and forgiving. To torture me
seemed sadistic. "Here's another whopper, Janet! What
are you gonna do with this one - screw up again or pass
this time?" No, the God I know would never test me. So
what in God's name was He doing?

One day, as I struggled in desperation, I noticed
Father standing before me - black and white striped shirt,
Nike sneakers laced neatly in a perfect bow, and a shiny
silver whistle suspended from a nylon chord around his
neck – Coach God. There I was, standing in the middle
the field looking like a deer in headlights. All the other
players were running widely around me, yelling and
screaming, kicking and throwing. *What the…?* Suddenly,
Coach called over to me, "Janet, wake up! Are you in this
game or not?" He must have sensed I was suffering from
FBS, *Foggy Brain Syndrome*, if you will (and even if you
won't – doesn't matter).

"Sweetheart, pay attention! You did sign up to play
in this game, didn't you? Your name's right here on my
roster. Life - it's called The Game of Life." (Some play
the board game but this one's for real.) "You wanted to
play and I'm here to show you how. I have the big book of
rules right here." In His right hand He held a large tablet,
(similar to the Sony Galaxy but not electronic, more of

the stone genre). Inscribed on the cover were the words "The Game of Life's Top Ten Rules".

"You can't dilly-dally. This game moves quickly and you'll get crushed if you don't pay attention." "But I have no idea what to do?" I stammered. (Oh me of little faith!) He smiled tenderly. "That's why I'm here. As your Coach, I'll teach you how to play. I'll guide and direct you throughout the entire game. I'm on your side and I want to you to win - big time. Just follow my rules, all of my rules, every time, the ones here in my original *galaxy* tab and you'll be fine."

"But what about all those people who cheat and don't play fair? How do I deal with them?" I questioned.

"You don't", He instructed. "Not everyone will play by the rules. Some will lie and steal and others will try to sabotage your efforts. Do not concern yourself with them. If you take your eye off the game for even a split second, you could get hurt. I have instant replay on my video cam. I review all tapes when the game is over and at the appropriate time will tend to those who haven't played nice."

"*I want you to win - big time.*" God's words resonated in my head. God is on my side. I don't have all the answers but He does. So all I have to do is trust my Coach, follow the rules of the game, and I'll win. In the Game of Life, I will emerge victorious - guaranteed! Not bad. In fact, it doesn't get any better than that.

> "I know the plans I have for you," declares the Lord. "Plans to prosper you and not harm you, plans to give you hope and a future." ~ Jeremiah 29:11

If the Truth Fits

Mother Theresa invites us to rethink they way we live our lives. Are we willing to abandon the road most frequently traveled which focuses on ego and personal desires? Are we willing to run enthusiastically into the arms of Father, committing ourselves wholeheartedly to His way? Are we fully prepared to redefine the meaning of life?

Are we ready to relinquish the belief that life is about me in relation to the rest of the world and recognize it is solely about God? My time in this world provides the opportunity for me to come to know my Creator fully and develop an unbreakable bond with Him. I can only accomplish this when I am fully willing to live my life according to His teachings, to be who He created me to be, to put forth exclusive effort in pleasing Him, and to disregard my status in this world. This realization opened my eyes to Truth.

A Really Smart (Oxy) Moron

Ok, remember earlier when I made that infuriating statement that for sure, my life is not about you? (By the way, thank you for not calling my mother.) Even though my life is not about you it *is* about you. (There you go again - another one of those oxymorons.) Here's why - God is *within you* so when my life is for *Him*, it is for *you* as well. When I live my life in Love, all whom I encounter reap the benefits. I speak from a place of Love. I treat all people with kindness. I seek to be of assistance not only to those I know and care about but to my many undiscovered friends also (aka strangers). I am tender and gentle and forgiving. I am indifferent to skin color, level of education, financial

> "Let all that you do be done in love." ~ 1 Corinthians, 16:14

status, limitations and afflictions, and country of origin.
I manifest the Divine.

I see as God sees, I speak as God speaks, I love as God loves.

~

Detour Along The Yellow Brick Road

This awareness was even more profound than I initially realized.

I began to contemplate all of the bad things that happened in my life beginning with my divorce. How did this *me and God* consciousness apply? After all, He wasn't responsible for the suffering and injustice I endured. That was definitely between me and the other parties. He gave us free will and each of us is responsible for the choices we make and the consequences or rewards that follow.

I remember with great clarity my initial reaction the day my husband left - I instinctively cried out to God for help. "Oh God, please help me," I pleaded through my tears. "I can't do this. I can't live without him. He is my life! I beg you – don't take him away from me!" (I knew God was not removing my husband from my life. He left of his own volition.) I was frightened and weak. I lacked confidence. I was without hope. I couldn't fathom how I could possible raise four young children on my own. How was I going to pay the bills and take care of a big house and yard on my own? What was I supposed to do if my car needed to be repaired? Who was I going to cuddle with in bed each night? My mind raced with anxiety as adrenaline pumped through my body.

I directed my children into the family car and headed off to church. I had trouble focusing on Mass. I didn't hear a word the priest was saying. Tears scorched my eyes like flames to dry leaves. Each day for the next six months, I returned to the sanctuary of my Father's house. I experienced a great sense of relief within those brick walls. Silent prayer connected me with Father's love and wisdom. Like a child reaching for her daddy's hand in the dark, He soothed my fears. His gentle arms lifted my spirits, His tender words filled my soul with strength, and His love comforted my aching heart. Gradually, I realized I was not alone, something I had been taught in my early days in Sunday school. The difference was now I could *feel* His presence.

A Catholic Walks Into a Presbyterian Church...

There is an even greater reason why all of life's challenges, experiences, losses, heartaches, disappointments, injustices, and mean-spirited people appear in our lives. Each presents a unique opportunity to come to know the heart of God. Many years ago, I was in the West Milford Presbyterian Church in (you guessed it) beautiful West Milford, N.J. Along the walls were taped handmade posters, each pronouncing an inspirational message from God. One in particular resonated with me. *"If you never hurt, how would you know that I will heal you?"* Oh my God - that's brilliant! The Bible clearly tells us *about* God. But how can we *know* God, really know Him, unless He comes through on His promises?

> *It is in the darkness of night that we see the brilliant light of the stars.*
> *It is in the darkness of our suffering that we see the brilliant Light of God's Heart.*

Find God in suffering

BFF's Forever

I am blessed to have several best friends - Denise, Arlene, Michelle, Leanne - some of whom have been in

Sample

my life for more than forty-five years. Each is wonderful, kind, loving, and supportive. Each on some level has conveyed that they would do anything for me. "If you ever need anything, just call. I'm here for you." How fortunate I am to have friends of such caliber. But how do I know they are women of integrity? Only under the most desperate of conditions is one's true character revealed.

Two o'clock in the morning is not the most convenient time to call a friend on the phone. But that's exactly the time I desperately needed to talk to someone. I dialed Arlene's number knowing full-well she was snug and sound asleep in her bed. Her greeting was barely audible. "Arlene, I'm so sorry to wake you up but I really need to come over and talk. I can't stop crying. I feel like I'm losing it." "I'll put on some tea," she replied. No huffing and puffing or moaning, no chastising me for calling at such an ungodly hour, nor complaints of having to get up in a few short hours for work (certainly all justifiable reasons for denying my request). Instead, she simply responded with love and concern. Her reply solidified our relationship. I knew she means what she says. That evening confirmed what I already knew - I could trust this friend with my life.

So it is with our relationship with our Creator. Words are cheap. Actions reveal. And God's character is revealed each time we reach out to Him and He fulfills His promise.

> "Be strong and courageous. Do not be afraid or terrified because of them, for the LORD your God goes with you; He will never leave you nor forsake you." ~ Deuteronomy 31:6

God of Alcatraz

Many of us come to know the heart of God upon finding ourselves in the darkest caverns of our lives - the diagnosis of a life-threatening illness, the loss of a child, incarceration or an addiction to a harmful substance or behavior. It is easy to overlook God's presence in our lives when all is well. We buy a luxury car and show it off to our family and friends, we invite our neighbors to watch four hours of video from our recent vacation to an exotic island, we bask in the latest award bestowed upon us for achieving a life-long goal or we celebrate the grand opening of new business. A quick "Thanks, God" or "God is good!" may emerge from our lips but in prosperous times He is, at best, a fleeting thought as we quickly move on to the next event.

Yet in times of pain and fear, we become acutely aware of His presence in our lives and more dependent upon Him for guidance, understanding, support, comfort, and healing. Our needs are great and only One of great ability and love is able to fulfill such requests. He is that One.

It is not uncommon to hear stories of criminals imprisoned for committing unspeakable crimes against humanity who claim to have *found God*. Many doubt their sincerity. "Who are they kidding? They ruin the lives of the innocent and then claim they now know God? That's ridiculous! Why now? Why not *before* they hurt all those people?" Why now? Because they, like the rest of us, lived in ego. Their lives revolved around themselves - what they wanted, how they were hurt or what they believe they are deserving of. They were profoundly disconnected from Spirit. We've all been-there-done-that on some level. Theirs was to the extreme.

It is often in their loneliness and despair that they begin to seek that which has been missing in their lives - a relationship with Spirit. In desperate need of healing the demons inhabiting their souls, in their loneliness, and those moments of fear and solitude with no source of love present to them, they turn to the One they instinctively know is omnipresent, the One who can and will heal them and restore them to wholeness.

A Million to None

One of my clients at the battered women's shelter I work at was a former multi-millionaire. The passing of her husband several years prior left her financially secure, or so she thought. Jet-setting around the world and living in luxury, her life revolved around the latest in fashion and cars, extravagant vacations, and expensive furs. Who had time for God? She had to be at the airport by 8:15 to catch her flight to Belize. Not heeding the advice of her financial manager, she squandered her fortune fulfilling her selfish whims. In a few short years, she filed bankruptcy, lost her home and all of her possessions, and ended up on the steps of the shelter with nothing more than a black garbage bag containing a few items of clothing.

Angry and uncooperative, she was terrified at what life held in store for her. "I've never worked a day in my life!" she confided in me. "I have no clue what I'm supposed to do now." Over the next few months, I spent many hours talking with her about her faith. "I have none. I lost everything! There is no God, at least not for me. If He really did exist, He would never have allowed this to happen to me." (I really had my work cut out for me but "Leslie" was a quick learner.) I shared my life's journey with her and although it was noticeably different from hers, there were striking similarities. We both sustained unexpected and significant losses. In my case, I relied on God to guide and direct me through the maze of uncertainties and fears. I relayed the impact choice had in my life. Gradually, she began to see God around her.

Most of our residents come from inner cities filled with violence and poverty yet there is a sisterhood of support that exists among them. Quick to share their last cigarette or Pampers, they watch out for the well-being of one another. They took Leslie under their wing. At first she was reluctant, because in her mind they were beneath her. Yet their generosity softened her heart as she gradually learned from their resiliency. She began to appreciate the little things - a donation of shampoo from a local Rotary Club, a ride in a rusted van to the welfare office, food stamps, and job training. She began to see God working miracles for her through others. Hope replaced despair, gratitude erased resentment, and faith replaced anger. Eventually, Leslie found employment at a local supermarket, received a donated car with 120,000 miles on it, and got her first-ever one bedroom apartment. I kept in touch with her for a long time after. She had never been happier in her life. Content with God's love and all the blessings He bestowed on her, she had, for the first time in her life, found inner peace. She had discovered the heart of God.

The Wicked Witch of Wayne

Lest you think I have come to know the heart of God through the suffering and pain inflicted upon me by others, understand it is also due to the anguish and agony I have imposed upon others, most notably my children. I was not always a candidate for *Mother of the Year*. Do I love my children? Absolutely, as much as any other mother. And like all parents who love their children, we sometimes treat them poorly. Though not intentional, the hurt we cause them is hurt none-the-less. (If I step on your toe accidently or purposefully, does it not cause as much pain?) There were times I was angry, unfair, and even cruel. I inadvertently took out my frustration and personal issues on them. I was (and this is putting in mildly) not a nice person. Ask them. They'll tell you. The old adage, "you always hurt the ones you love" was perfected by me (not a Guinness record I'm proud of). I was ravaged with shame and guilt. The sight of my own reflection in the bedroom mirror disgusted me. My self-imposed moniker was the *Wicked Witch of Wayne.*

How could this be happening? This was not me! I have never in my life been a mean or cruel person and to hurt my children - that is the most vile and contemptible atrocity imaginable. Mothers are supposed to protect and nurture their offspring. While at times I excelled at motherhood, other times I resembled Jekyll and Hyde. I was terrified and lost. I didn't know where or who to turn to so I turned to the One who was always present. I poured out my heart to Him. I cried out for help. Through a series of Divine connections, He brought me to Mary, my therapist for many years to come. A striking reflection of God, Mary was one of the most gifted and spiritual women I've ever known. Through her guidance, support, compassion, and love, I was able to identify the deeply rooted issues that caused me to act out so abhorrently against my children and to address and eventually heal them. She spent long months helping me rebuild my fragile self-esteem and learn to love and forgive myself for the mistakes I had made.

The time I spent in Mary's presence was time spent in the presence of God. She radiated unconditional love and her genuine concern for my emotional and spiritual well-being allowed me to trust her implicitly. Through meditative exercises which she instructed me to practice, I began developing a relationship with God in a way I had never experienced before. Alone in His presence, I was able to actually *feel* His sacred love and for the first time in my life, felt complete.

The Space Between Me and God

My newfound realization that life has nothing at all to do with others was in essence a spiritual rebirth. I felt as though I had been born for the first time, not into my human life as I had well over half a century ago, but rather reborn back to Spirit. I no longer saw myself as a human being but rather one of Spirit temporarily inhabiting a physical body. My sole purpose in life was not about fulfilling all of *my* hopes and dreams. Those were pleasant enough goals. My life took on new meaning - it was to come to know the heart of God. That's it, plain and simple. Dr. Steve McSwain, author of the award-winning <u>The Enoch Factor</u>, (one of my top ten all-time favorite books) says, "To know God is the supreme purpose of every human being." Brilliant man. I couldn't agree more.

I didn't always have to be right. Things didn't have to go my way. People didn't have to like me or approve of me. I didn't have to have everything I want or dream of. I didn't have to accomplish great things or earn tons of money in order to be important or to have value.

All God asks of me is to align my heart with His, to know Him on a deeply intimate level and reflect His presence in this world so that others may know Him as well.

Every experience and every individual who enters my life (especially the problematic ones) provide that opportunity for me. The polite, kind, and helpful people are easy to deal with. It takes no effort to be kind in kind. It is not difficult to care for or love them. But remember - Olympic gold medals aren't awarded to those who gingerly somersault across a big foam mat. And you don't align with the heart of the Almighty by engaging in acts of kindness that take minimal effort. Don't get me wrong - every act of love and benevolence is noticed, appreciated, and rewarded. But the real challenge to know and grow lies within the most demanding encounters.

The angry, self-centered people, the know-it-alls, those who are prejudice or racist, the murderers, rapists, and child abusers - with each God asks me to respond to them as He would, with love and compassion, guidance, and forgiveness. If I respond in kind, does that not only reinforce what they already know and live - anger, abuse, and prejudice? God's way provides the opportunity to come to know the the Father as I have.

> ### *I am called to be a messenger of God's love and healing to each of His wounded children.*

The first line of the Prayer of St. Francis of Assisi says, "Lord, make me an instrument of your peace."

> ### *Peace is the very essence of God's heart.*

If I am able to bring peace to all whom I encounter, I have the opportunity to facilitate dramatic change on a global level. Granted, this is not for the faint-of-heart. It takes great strength and devotion to God's Word to love those who hate, to reach out to those who abuse, and to forgive those who murder.

> "But I say unto you, Love your enemies, bless them that curse you, do good to them that hate you, and pray for them which despitefully use you and persecute you." ~ Matthew 5:44

The Amish and Kidneys

On Oct. 1, 2006, in Nickel Mine, Pa., Charles Carl Roberts walked into an elementary school and shot and killed five young Amish girls before turning the gun on himself. The Amish community stunned the world by announcing they had forgiven the man who took the lives of their children. Relying on the teachings of their Bible, they chose to do good to their enemy and not return evil for evil. When asked if the shooter's wife would be welcome among them, they replied affirmatively. Amidst tragedy, they exemplified the Father's Love and compassion for all His children. Who among us could honestly say we have within us the desire to follow God's teachings under such gruesome conditions?

> *His Way is not the easy way,*
> *but His Way is the easy way.*
> *His Way is not our way,*
> *yet His Way must be our way.*

I have never lost a love one through a deliberate act of physical violence. Yet I have had loving relationships destroyed due to vicious rumors and false accusations perpetuated by jealous vindictive people. The losses were excruciatingly painful and completely unjustifiable. Yet in each instance, I chose not only to forgive in my heart but also continue to treat each person with dignity and respect. I chose never to allow anyone to change who I am. And let me just say, this is not without considerable effort at times. But I am a child of God and as God's offspring I must behave in a loving manner *no matter what.* Is it acknowledged and appreciated by those being revered? No. Is it reciprocated? No, but that is of no importance. Remember, this is between *me and God*, it is not about *them*, even though they will benefit if they so choose.

There was one person in particular who caused me such pain as to almost end my life as I know it. Their reasons were purely selfish and spiteful. Over the course of time, not only was I able to forgive them but I also chose to continue to love them as I always had. I have not a single feeling of animosity towards them nor does the thought of them suffering for their actions bring me satisfaction. In fact, the contrary is true. I do not want any harm to come to them in any way. What I pray for is their healing. If this person was dying and in need of a kidney, and mine was the only perfect match, I wouldn't hesitate. After all, God gave us, even the hateful sinners, His Beloved Son. Surely a kidney is not asking too much. To reach a place of unconditional love and forgiveness is not always an easy journey but it is certainly attainable and definitely worth every effort.

I am here to embody the heart of God.

In all situations, with all people, in every word spoken, and in every action taken, I must ask myself, "Am I a messenger of Love?" Do I consistently mirror God's presence in this world? When my heart becomes one with the 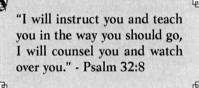 Source of Love, God is pleased with me and I achieve a state of inner peace.

> "I will instruct you and teach you in the way you should go, I will counsel you and watch over you." - Psalm 32:8

26.2 Miles of Agony

Knowing that suffering is meant to show us the compassion nature of God's heart, I do not need to fear or resist it. Upon recognizing its necessity and purpose, my pain ceases. As I mentioned earlier, I competed in two race-walking marathons in my forties. The two-month training period was grueling but I did not agonize over it. I knew it was a necessary process towards realizing my ultimate goal. I willingly arose each Saturday at three AM to embark on a four or five-hour workout.

Sweat, sore muscles, and blisters were all endured without complaint. The glory of crossing the finish line, accompanied by the gold medals I won, made the entire process worthwhile.

Subsequently, I can remove angst for the suffering others face as I now understand, even though they may not, that it is essential in their personal journey toward knowing God. Rather than trying to alleviate it or suffer along with them, I can be at peace and pray they will discover what I (and you) now know.

I have a loved one on such a journey. She is struggling with deep personal issues and is sadly ruining her life. Not willing to listen to or receive help from those who care about her, her life and happiness have rapidly deteriorated. Her entire family is suffering as a result. Many have abandoned her. Not I - I pray for her awareness and openness to God's Love. I pray she allows Him into her heart to heal all of her pain and distress and to restore her to wholeness. The knowledge that this is all necessary for her spiritual growth comforts me to a certain degree.

5/9/19

Defining Moment 3

I'm not certain in what order Defining Moment 3 appeared in my life. It may have preceded Moment 2. Either way, it is of no less importance. I distinctly remember it occurred in May of 2001.

P-ew!

My oldest grandson, then seven, was making his First Holy Communion. He and my daughter had only recently re-entered my life, an event my ex was less than enthusiastic about. Being in church for this celebration would be the first time in nearly six years he and I would be in close proximity to one another. Needless to say, my daughter was a bit apprehensive. To ease the anxiety for everyone (I was fine with the situation), she arranged to have her father and I seated at opposite ends of the pew with at least a dozen people situated between us.

I arrived early as usual and sat in my assigned seat. As each subsequent family member arrived, I moved down one seat, then another, and another. (Can you see where I'm going with this?) A moment before Mass began, he entered through the side door of the church and sought out our family pew. Lo-and-behold, the only remaining seat was the one directly adjacent to me. He gingerly lowered himself onto the darkened oak bench, careful not to make body contact - probably because I have cooties. (Remember cooties? If you keep your fingers crossed, you can't catch them. Maybe I should have reminded him.)

Anyhow… near the end of Mass, the priest asked the congregation to turn to those around us and offer one another a sign of God's peace. Being Italian, I usually greet those nearest me with a big hug. For those less familiar, a handshake is more appropriate. As the moment approached, I was uncertain as to how to handle this sensitive situation. So I prayed to God. "What do you want me to do, Lord?" I asked. In my right ear, God's voice clearly responded, "Why would I want you to treat him any differently than anyone else?" *Good answer*, I thought. (Like God's going to give me a stupid answer?) I thought a hug might not be well received so I extended my hand. "Peace be with you," I stated. He definitely did not look comfortable. I think he mumbled something similar and quickly turned away. (Sad, we used to be deeply in love and now he couldn't bear to casually touch my hand.) It was almost over – Mass, that is.

But we're not out of the woods yet. Oh, contraire! In a few moments we would begin praying the Our Father and would be asked to join hands with those next to us for the recitation of the entire prayer. Once again, I asked God for guidance. "What should I do now, Lord?" "Don't push it," He replied. So I quietly folded my hands in front of me as I began praying.

While this moment may not seem to be one of great importance, for me it was epic. I had been raised to be polite, kind, and considerate to everyone. And I would like to believe that for the better part of my life I have been. But at this precise instant, I realize how I treat others was in no way dependant on how they are treating me *nor how they felt about me or I about them*. I am required to extend the same courtesies to those who despise me as I do to those who revere me. In one fleeting but profound moment, I had a deeper understanding of how God wanted me to live my life. I must not concern myself with how others behave. I must maintain the highest level of integrity at all times. Rise above. Be the example. One seemingly insignificant instant transformed my life forever. If others ignore me, I will still address them. If they criticize me I will offer a compliment. If they blame me unjustly I will make them my friend.

Remember Matthew 5 - "... do good to them that hate you."

The Junior King

I am reminded of a famous quote of Dr. Martin Luther King, Jr. when addressing the issue of violence. He speaks of brutality and aggression as a cycle that must be broken. Someone, somewhere, he states, needs to be of such high moral integrity as to break the pattern of violence. To retaliate only perpetuates the cycle of hatred.

> ✦ **Hatred, bitterness, rudeness, and disrespect are all acts of emotional violence. Maintain your integrity. Rise above. Be the example.**

Bears repeating.

— need to have
your goodness
affirmed by
others

— need to have a
strong sense of self
— child of God
loved by God

find "my truth"

Holy Spirit — higher energy
Gifts of the Holy Spirit

CHAPTER 3

Ask Only This – Life's Most Defining Question

Red Sling Backs

The realization I exist *solely* to understand and be at one with the heart of God, thus allowing me to be a vessel for others to come to that same awareness, challenged me to question the choices I was making and the way I was living my life. Wanting to always make the best possible decisions (as we all do) I discovered I oftentimes lacked the proper knowledge to do so. How could I possibly know if marrying someone or having children was the right choice? How could I know if moving to another state or becoming friends with a particular individual was in my best interest? Could I be 100% certain I was making the right career choice? Discovering the answers to such diverse questions was daunting. There was no book written, no family member, friend or professional, no psychic, mystic or doctor who could definitively give me the accurate answer each and every time. Life was a hit-and-miss, trial-by-error, learn-as-you-go adventure. In smaller less important issues (Should I buy the black pumps or the red sling backs?) there was less concern on my part. If I regretted the purchase, I could return it. Or if I decided I didn't care for the shoes after wearing them, they could be donated to charity or passed on to a family member. No big deal.

The Happiness Hype

I was tired and frustrated from making poor choices in the more important areas of my life. The question "Will this make me happy?" didn't suffice. I could be happy in the moment, only to find sadness or regret at a later date or discover my happiness has caused suffering to another. (I'm ecstatic about my new hobby of antique collecting. However, this decision is putting a financial burden on my family.) My happiness was not the real issue. Trust me, there's way too much emphasis put on personal happiness. Read on - you'll see what I'm talking about.

I tried living my life in pursuit of my passion and I have many - nature, exercise, lecturing, writing, singing, photography, and a few more. So which path do I follow and what about an income? Certainly I needed to make a living so I could survive. Could I make a reasonable salary engaging in any of these? (I still haven't found anyone willing to pay me for power-walking.) I decided the logical approach was to determine what God put me here to do and follow my life's purpose. Surely that was the correct answer. In the early '90's I did just that - I wrote and published my first book, The Seedling's Journey, and began my career as a motivational speaker and author. I was delirious with joy. Still am.

So why, then, was I still frustrated, angry, hurt, lonely, and confused? These emotions were such a distraction to my happiness and the fulfillment of my goals. It occurred to me that I was concerning myself with the wrong things. If I made a bad decision, would people judge me? Would there be a backlash of criticism? If I was not a good enough wife, mother or friend would I be rejected and abandoned yet again? Are people rating my success by the price tag on my car and the size of my house? But why did any of that matter to me? If issues of this nature were causing me distress, I needed to re-evaluate what was really important.

"Me and God". "Me and God." These words preoccupied my thoughts and pursued me relentlessly day and night like a private eye trailing his suspect. I reminded myself that my life is solely about my relationship with my Creator. If I made a bad choice, what would *He* think? Wasn't that more relevant than other's opinions? What did *He* think about the money I spent on my car and my house? Was *He* pleased with my career choice? Was I the kind of mother, friend or sister *He* wanted me to be? *I need to concern myself only with pleasing God*, I thought. Isn't that exactly what I did in my third defining moment at my grandson's Communion? That incident had nothing at all to do with me or my ex. It was solely about doing what God asked me to do.

One-Hit-Wonder No More

Since the dawn of our existence, there have been dozens of philosophical questions burning in the mind of humanity - what is the meaning of life, why is there something rather than nothing, why did the chicken cross the road? (Opps, sorry. My mistake.) Ok, maybe not that last one but the others are certainly valid.

They challenge our capacity to reason and resolve as well as make for an interesting debate. While each may satisfy a curiosity and enrich our lives to some degree, they pale by comparison to the one essential question guaranteed to redirect the course of your life. (No, not *which came first – the chicken or the egg*, silly!). Four simple words, complied in query form that will:

- Enable you to manifest an authentic life based on moral integrity.
- Safeguard you from mistakes and errors.
- Allow you to rightly resolve every dilemma with unqualified veracity.
- Heal all wounds and preclude future suffering for all humankind (including the self).
- Experience unlimited joy and abundance.

While these claims may sound grandiose, they are far more unpretentious than one would imagine. I now know for certain that the answer to all of life's queries is contained in one simple four word question: "**Does This Please God?**"

> *The way to contentment and joy (far more important than happiness) is by living life in a manner pleasing to God.*

Before engaging in any thought process or behavior, inquire of Divine Source as to whether or not your forthcoming actions are favorable to Him.

That's it, plain and simple, end of story. Well, actually not that simple and it's just the beginning of the story. Modifying our behaviors to reflect God's presence in this world necessitates making sure every thought entertained, every word uttered, and every action taken is in alignment with who God is.

> *To reflect His existence in this world, to live in such a manner as to exemplify Spirit*

in human form, to enable others to feel the very presence of the Almighty is the epitome of sacredness.

~

There is no greater purpose or reward in life than to be God for others.

Philosophical Questions and Road Kill

Concerning myself with my own happiness is ego. Concentrating my efforts on pleasing God is Spirit. But accomplishing this is no easy task. How do I know for certain if a behavior, attitude or decision is agreeable to my Heavenly Father? How can one know for certain if He's satisfied with my choices? It is a query of epic proportion but then again, life is filled with provocative questions.

Regarding those philosophical matters we studied in high school and college: while many have not yet resolved these quandaries there is, in my mind, a more pressing query. Knowing *why there is something rather than nothing* may be interesting to discern but for me it does not impact the quality of my life. There *is something*, that's the fact so I deal with what is before me without necessarily having to know how or why it got there. And chickens cross the road all the time, although sometimes end up as road kill. Sad, but it's not a question I need to concern myself with at this time.

Isn't it rather presumptuous to think anyone could even remotely comprehend the mind of the Almighty and know emphatically what pleases Him? After all, we are mere mortals with severely limited intellects. How could one ever possibly fathom the mind of the

Omnipotent, the All-Perfect, All-Knowing Being, the One from whom all knowledge originates? To even suggest such an endeavor is on some level arrogant to say the least, wouldn't you agree?

① Presence of God

nature(walking)

CHAPTER 4

The Master('s) Mind

Heeeere's God!

In order to align one's mind with the mind of God, one must first know *who* God is. I am not referring to our intellectual understanding of who this Supreme Being is - "God is the Creator of the universe and all that is." "God is my Heavenly Father." "God is the first person in the Holy Trinity." Sunday school knowledge introduces us to our Heavenly Father and encourages a relationship with Him. We can read the Bible and learn of His benevolence and the many miracles He performed. We are told of His power and might, His unconditional love, and unfaltering generosity. But knowing facts about God in our heads is a far cry from *knowing* God. One must come to know the *heart* of God in order to even begin to understand the *mind* of the Father.

One of my best friends is a beautiful woman named Michelle. She is pretty, classy, kind, and generous, loyal, trustworthy, and smart, Michelle is a woman of integrity. I could go on and on. Would you know who she is simply by my reveling certain facts or perceptions of her? Of course not. You would know *about* her but you would not *know* her. To truly know who Michelle is, you would need to experience her, build a relationship with her, and witness her in her authentic personhood.

So it is with God. Intellectual knowledge does not suffice. Spending time with Him and experiencing Him is quite another thing. But how does one accomplish that? Where does one even begin? Finding God is not that difficult.

In Nature

First, God is easily found in Nature. After all, He created the trees, streams, animals, and stars. He *is* Nature. Spending time alone in the environment allows us to experience the perfection of God. Look closely - everything in Nature is flawless. Nothing needs to be improved upon. No one has to get up in the morning and plug Nature in. No one needs to tell the sun to shine or the wind to blow. Nature instinctively knows when to lower temperatures or raise them. There is no waste in Nature, either. She automatically recycles everything. There were no instructions written on how to do that nor ordinances passed making it mandatory. Nature knows precisely when to create life in one form and transition it to another.

Nature is not jealous - nothing compares itself to another. No one has ever witnessed a rose bush complain how unfair it is that the oak tree down the road is much taller or how it violates the rose's civil rights. Neither has the shrub taken its case to the Supreme Court seeking a six-figure settlement for prejudice or extreme emotional distress.

Nature isn't vengeful either. Just because I have poisoned my parcel of land with harmful toxins, she doesn't retaliate by releasing an over abundance of snow in my yard the following winter (well, maybe with the exception of Jan. of '95). She maintains her integrity and continues to do what Nature was designated to do.

Nature does not play favorites - streams are cared for as lovingly as spiders, mountains as tenderly as clouds, and rocks are considered as precious as toadstools.

And nature has never engaged in war - she knows only harmony. There is no animosity or prejudice, no religion or nationality, no race or class, and no winning or losing. Equality and fairness govern all of Nature's activities.

Perfection only creates - never destroys.

Nature does not grieve. In all her wisdom, she fully understands the cycle of life and recognizes that nothing ends but merely transitions form. Therefore, there is no need for sadness and no reason to mourn. There is only acceptance of what is destined to be.

And Nature is beauty – whether it is the dry sands of the Sahara or the monsoons of South America, an ordinary garden snake or a rare albino chipmunk, an odorous skunk or fragrant lilac bush. That which is created in perfection is magnificent.*

I have always felt at one with Nature and have spent countless hours basking in her wonder. For me, it has been fairly easy to develop a deeper awareness of God through her.

In Others

Nature is not the only means available to experience God. God resides in each and every one of us. So to

---

* (Read "Garden of Weedin" @ http://www.pfeiffer powerseminars.com/pps1-newsletter.html#weedin)

come to appreciate who He is, it is imperative to see Him in those we encounter. This is not always easy as many conceal Him behind an opaque shroud of bad attitudes and behaviors. But He resides within regardless.

We have all encountered people who radiate love and kindness. My mom is one of them. You cannot be in her company without feeling the presence of God. Kind, sweet, generous, and loving – there is not a malicious bone in her body. She radiates peace and forgiveness - her life is a living example of God's infinite goodness. One cannot help but become a better person for having known her. She inspires others to be more loving and has a natural ability to effortlessly bring out the "God-ness" in them.

Even those with less that Godly behavior - upon closer examination it is possible to see a glimmer of goodness, a spark of kindness or a radiance of love within. Keep searching. It's there. And perhaps, you can even help them bring it forth.

In Children

Ring Around the (Toilet) Bowl

I love little children. There's an innocence about them as they radiate God's light. I think back to a time when my children were young - Rich was three, his younger sister, Toni, was two. Both were out of diapers when they went into the bathroom together to take care of business. A few moments later, I checked to make sure everything was ok. There was my little girl standing in front of the commode crying. "What happened?" I asked. She appeared to be fine. "I dropped my ring in the toilet", she sobbed as she pointed her tiny finger towards the porcelain bowl. "Don't worry, sweetheart," I said. "I'll get you another one next time we go to the supermarket." (The plastic trinket came from a gumball machine at

Pathmark.) But before I could dry her tears, her big brother valiantly reached in and retrieved her prized possession. I gasped in horror as he pulled her gumball jewelry to safety! Her face lit up with glee. "Thanks, Rich," her tiny voice echoed joyfully. He shrugged his shoulders as though it was no big deal. This is what big brothers do – make things right for their little sister.

> "Except ye become as little children, ye will not enter the Kingdom of Heaven."
> ~ Matthew 18:3

So it is with God's love for us - in the great toilet bowl of life, no matter how much sh*t we get ourselves into, He will reach in and save us without a moment's hesitation. Never would it enter His mind to pull the handle and *flush* even the least of us, no matter how *plastic* we behave. For in His eyes, in the mind and heart of God, we are all equally as priceless as a VSS diamond from Tiffany's. (Ok, maybe that's not the best analogy but you get the picture. Sorry if I grossed anyone out. No more potty humor, I promise.)

> "Never will I leave you; never will I forsake you." So say with confidence, "The Lord is my helper; I will not be afraid."
> ~ Hebrews 13:5, 6

Children have a great advantage over those of us who have been in this life for ....well, a very long time. In their innocence they are still very much connected to the Divine and exemplify His pure nature. They live with carefree abandon, love freely and effortlessly, are eager to please, and quick to forgive. They are eternally optimistic and believe in the unseen and the impossible. (Ever known a child who didn't think they could fly?) They marvel at the most mundane things (a dandelion puff) and see beauty where adults see yucky (centipedes). They hope in all things and imagine the unimaginable. They find humor in everything, especially belching, and sadness quickly dissipates with someone tripping over their shoelace.

In Dogs

Either Way It Spells Love

And then, of course, there are *dogs*. (You do know that DoG spelled backwards is GoD? That's not a coincidence by the way.) There is so much one can learn about God by observing His canine alter-ego. To know a dog is to know love. There are no limits to their capacity for affection. One of my canine babies, Halle, was rescued from animal research. Abused and left caged 24/7 for the first seven years of her life, Halle came to me in the fall of 2003. Malnourished, terrified, dirty, and with sores all over her body, she embodied God's perfect Love. From the moment I met her, she showered me with unconditional devotion and loyalty. I never questioned her love for me. No matter how badly she had been treated prior, her past was quickly replaced with her intense desire to love and be loved. Nothing else mattered to her (with the exception of kibble). She never complained about the unfair treatment she received, sought revenge on those who brutally tortured and experimented on her or harbored resentment. Like most dogs I've met, Halle's eagerness to give love and be loved was her primary concern. If the activity wasn't fun, happy or tasty, Halle didn't engage in it.

So how do any of the above assist us in knowing God?

First, look at **Nature** - she's fair, confident, forgiving, peaceful, radiates beauty, celebrates every facet of life, and loves equally.

Others - they reach out to total strangers when natural disasters strike, donate hours of personal time to volunteer work, choose helping careers to improve the lives of others, comfort a crying child who's tennis ball went down the sewer drain, and contribute billions of dollars to charities and non profits.

Children - love freely and effortlessly, are eager to please, and quick to forgive. They are optimistic, carefree, and find wonder and beauty in everything imaginable. They forgo sadness for joy in every instance.

Dogs - forgiving, lovable and loving, playful and loyal to a fault, never complain, are eager to please, and will lay down their life for the one they love. (Remind you of anyone you know? Hint - it begins with the letter *J* and rhymes with *please us*.)

Thus is the nature of God. His mind contemplates all that is good, holy, and pure. Anything and everything *love-based* resides within His mind.

Is It *Me*?

Let me clarify - it is important to remember that the question is, "**Does *This* Please God?**" not "Do *I* Please God?" God is always pleased with me. After all, I am His child - the love of His life. He adores me without reservation. My behaviors, choices, and actions, however, are quite a different story. God is certainly not pleased with some of the shenanigans I've pulled during my life, like the time I pushed my little sister backwards off the swing. She wouldn't give me a chance on that particular one. When she fell to the ground, hitting her head and losing her breath, I felt awful. I hurt her and made her cry. The fact that there were three other identical swings on that frame didn't matter to me. I wanted *that* one and in my immature mind if she didn't give it up, well, I'd just have to take it.

In the New York Times #1 bestseller, <u>The Shack</u> (Wm. Paul Young), the main character, Mackenzie, speaks with God who reassures him that because God has no expectations of us other than what He already knows about us, we can never disappoint Him. (Like a parent who knows his child hasn't yet perfected walking –there is no disappointment when the child falls.) So it is with Father - always pleased with *me*, not so much with the way I act.

Know that behavior is not who we are - it is a learned response to a situation. It is an outward expression of what we are dealing with internally. Behavior expresses what I am *feeling* but it is not who I *am*. Intrinsically I am perfect. (Remember we have all been created in the image and likeness of the Father who is without fault.) My behavior may be inappropriate or offensive but I can unlearn what is not acceptable and relearn something far more suitable.

This is a critical distinction to make because it enables us to be less judgmental of others. "He's an idiot!" becomes "I'm really angry at that ridiculous statement he made." (*He* devalues the individual, *what he said* addresses the behavior.) How often do we diminish one's self-worth and fail to recognize it is what they are saying or doing that we are upset about? Judging others contradicts God's nature. He does not judge. He understands our imperfections just as a mother does who patiently waits for her child to learn to drink from a cup without spilling the contents.

> "Judge not lest ye be judged."
> ~ Matthew 7:1

Stop !

Avalanche of Esteem

Questioning whether or not God is pleased with *me* can take its toll on one's self-esteem. If, for even one moment, I doubt God's unconditional love and acceptance of me then my mind tells me there is something innately wrong with me – Janet, the person. And if God cannot love what He has created and who is an extension of His glory, then who in this imperfect world could ever find me worthy? People continually find fault with one another and are overly critical at times. So it is imperative for my emotional well-being to know, unequivocally, there is one Supreme Being who recognizes my worth despite the mistakes and errors I make.

I am a mother of four, grandmother of a lot and still counting. I see the beauty and wonder in each of my children and their children. Nothing could ever cause me to turn away from them. But I have witnessed some behaving in ways I am not always pleased with. I've seen them make choices I would have preferred they didn't make.

I have lost my patience and become angry with them at times. That is part of my human deficiency. But nothing diminishes the love I feel for them or lessens the value of who they are. That remains constant and unchanged. They could never do or say anything that would cause me to love or cherish them less. And the love our Heavenly Father feels for us is infinitely greater than that which we feel for our own offspring.

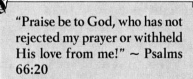

> "Praise be to God, who has not rejected my prayer or withheld His love from me!" ~ Psalms 66:20

God's In Love   6/13/19

God sees through the eyes of love, incessantly reflecting on the goodness and splendor in each of

His precious children. He is quick to forgive - offering understanding rather than judgment.

It's reminiscent of one's state of mind when they fall in love - all that person sees in their beloved is beauty. Blinded to their imperfections and fiercely protective, they defend their loved one from any perceived harm and are quick to excuse any transgressions. Patience, understanding, forgiveness, and support are all elements of being *in love*.

So it is with God - eternally infatuated with each of us, fiercely protective, and understanding to a fault.

His mind is incapable of bitterness, fear, jealously, resentment, arrogance, and such. Negative emotions are reserved for the human experience and are not inherent in Divine Nature. They do, in fact, cause a separation between the minds - ours and Divine - and disconnect us from our Source of Oneness. One must synchronize one's own mind with the mind of the Divine in order to live in harmony.

Violins, Ponies and Surfing

Look at it this way - an orchestra consists of many different instruments, each playing their own part of the symphony. If each musician thinks as an individual, separate and apart from the unit, then violins and clarinets are competing in a cacophony of noise, loosing sight of the function of the orchestra. Only when each performer listens to and aligns their instrument to that of the whole does the composition resonate in perfect harmony.

When I was a teenager, I spent many years riding horses. My instructor, Sgt. James Gannon, trained horses for the N.Y. City police department and also worked with Olympic equestrians. Sarge instructed us to become one with the horse and to align our mind with that of our steed. In that way, we functioned as one unit, in perfect harmony, as opposed to two separate entities at odds with one another.

One mind, single purpose, effortless motion.

My son, Rich, is a surfer. Speaking about his time in the ocean, he explained that in order to be proficient in this sport he must become one with the waves and think as a wave might think. In that way, the ride is exhilarating and glorious. To disconnect can prove disastrous.

Align with the Divine

A simple reminder to always think and be at one with God is to remind your self to *Align with the Divine.* When I reside in Oneness, I am whole and happy, life is effortless, and I reap immeasurable rewards. Only when I disconnect and think and behave in my mortal state do I create pain and suffering for myself and (very often) those around me as well.

> "The kingdom of God is within you." ~ Luke 17:21

~

"Align with the Divine."

~ *"Oneness"*

"As the mind of God thinks, so does mine."

God is gentle and patient. He does not force but tenderly and consistently encourages. When He sees one of His children broken and behaving badly, He seeks to guide them back to the path of Truth. His focus is always to elicit the goodness in each of us, seeking ways to restore us to Oneness with Him. This is referred to as *atonement* (at-one-ment), to make reparation or amends, to return to harmony with the One.

Punishment and vengeance contradict His very nature. He longs for us to learn but does not force lessons upon us. Rather, He allows us to seek out knowledge and delights when we do. Humans are the only species who feel compelled to teach one another a lesson when someone does not conform to their dictates. This creates a wedge between the self-proclaimed teacher and God because it is out of alignment with Divine - it contradicts the heart of God. We have all experienced frustration and anger when trying to teach someone a lesson. Let go. Patiently encourage them as they come to the realization in their own time and way.

Floral Egos

I have two acres of beautifully landscaped property with colorful gardens. In each, I've planted a wide array of flora - roses, tulips, chrysanthemums, geraniums, daisies, sweet Williams, peonies, and others whose names elude me. One day, while preparing dinner in the kitchen, I heard voices outside. I wasn't expecting company or the UPS guy so I ventured outside to see who was there. No one was visible yet the voices continued. I followed them around to the front of my house. Still no one. I stood for a moment wondering if perhaps I needed medication for those voices in my head when suddenly I heard sounds emanating from below. I looked down and realized they were coming from my garden.

"What the heck is wrong with you? Are you lazy or just plain stupid? Here it is June and I'm already in full bloom and you've barely stuck your head out of the ground. Loser!" I couldn't believe what was happening!

My garden was at war with itself! I stood in disbelief as the not-so-sweet williams and geraniums argued, criticizing one another and calling each other vile names. I was horrified!

"What in the world is going on here?" I questioned. What was supposed to be a diverse assortment of vibrant plant life turned into a battle ground of floral egos. "Rose" explained that while she was in full bloom, her lazy cohorts were dilly-dallying and not taking this whole garden thing seriously. "The growing season doesn't last forever, you know," she remarked sarcastically.

"Hold on a minute", I said. "It's not up to you to determine how and when each flower should grow. The growing conditions must be ideal for each of you and every one has a unique set of criteria. You, my friend, do not get to dictate the growth patterns of Daisy, Peony or any of the others. Your role is to be the best _you_ and leave the rest up to Nature. One does not demand flowers bloom. They must be nurtured and supported and appreciated at each stage of their growth. That's God's way."

Ok, I must confess. This didn't actually happen and no, I don't hear voices (at least not from my garden). But I wanted to illustrate an important point. Wouldn't it be completely absurd if, in fact, nature behaved in such a childish and arrogant manner? We all know that everything in nature has a time and place and one cannot and must not force her to conform to our expectations.

> "To every thing there is a season, and a time to every purpose under the heaven"
> ~ Ecclesiastes 3:1

Nature expects nothing. It does not demand, reprimand or threaten. So it is with the nature of God. Man, considered to be the highest form of life on the planet (Really? Because sometimes it's not very apparent.), is the only one who violates this principle. When we impose demands on one another to be who we want them to be or do what we want and when we want, we create misery and suffering for all.

Again, God's mind is void of all expectations and demands and instead is filled with hope, love, patience, and understanding. Imagine for a moment, if you will, what your life would look like if you replaced your limited mindset with that of the Benevolent Divine?

The Village Voice

During one of Wayne Dyer's lectures I attended, he spoke of a village in a remote part of the world that uses a unique form of *discipline.* When one of their citizens commits an offense, rather than put him or her on trial and impose a sentence, the citizens place that individual in the center of town. Day after day, one by one, the villagers approach the wrongdoer. (No, they don't stone him. That's what some of you were thinking, wasn't it?) Instead of reprimanding him, they pay him homage or state something positive to him. He must remain seated until all residents have approached him. This could take several days or even a week. At the conclusion of his *sentence,* he is set free. Having had a multitude of praise and positive affirmations bestowed upon him, he experiences a transformation of heart.

This is God manifest on Earth, I thought - an absolute example of God's perfect love - and from a *primitive* culture none-the-less. (Maybe it's time to redefine *primitive.*)

Seven Quick Questions

Understanding how God thinks is one thing. Applying it to everyday situations and quandaries can pose quite a challenge. While I might believe I have a comprehensive grasp of this, how can I be absolutely certain? After all, as a human being I have limitations. And since no one I've ever known personally has actually spoken directly to God and had Him explain in great detail the workings of His mind, I may feel as though answering the question **"Does This Please God?"** is pure speculation.

Remembering that God is Love allows us to discern if our behavior is pleasing to Him. Here are a few questions to ask yourself before engaging in any action:

- Is what I'm about to say or do kind?
- Does it emanate from a place of love for all parties?
- Is it based on truth rather than speculation, lies, jealousies or my own insecurities?
- Does it care about the well-being of all those concerned?
- Does it take into consideration the feelings and needs of the other?
- Is it absolutely the best choice I can make at this time?
- Will it achieve long-lasting and far-reaching benefits for all those concerned?

A resounding "yes" to each of these questions is a strong indication our behavior will be favorable and pleasing to God and a good personal choice as well.

Too often in life, we fail to consider the above questions. At times, we delude ourselves into believing we can honestly

> "Love is patient, Love is kind, Love does not insist on its own way. Love bears all things, believes all things, hopes all things, endures all things. Love never fails." ~ Corinthians 13:4-8

respond to each with an emphatic "yes" when the truth is we have underlying issues or ulterior motives. A single parent denies the other visitation claiming the child is not safe with them or is better off without them. But in reality, the custodial parent is angry that their former partner is no longer grieving the breakup of their relationship and may have even moved on to loving another. In this situation, a parent who claims to love and protect their child is in fact being motivated by hurt, anger, bitterness, and jealousy. Most, if not all, of us live

> **"Then you will know the truth, and the truth will set you free."**
> **~ John, 8:32**

in denial for the better (or should I say *worse?*) part of our lives.

"Denial is not a river in Egypt. It is a black abyss of fear that keeps us imprisoned in false truths and obstructs our chances of achieving personal greatness."*

~

God is Truth and those who reside in Truth live unencumbered by life's relentless deceptions.

6/29/19   5 top.

What's In Your Heart?

Equally as important as our behavior is the sincerity in our hearts. Again, I exist in the human condition and therefore am fallible. Periodically, I am misled,

---

*   Janet Pfeiffer, United Nations, Oct. 6, 2004

misinformed, ignorant, fearful, pressured, weary or consumed with my own personal issues. I screw up, big time. Does this mean I'm a bad person? No, it means I've fallen short of God's way. I failed to live in Spirit, (Align with the Divine) and fell into ego - as Wayne Dyer says, *Edging God Out*. In essence, I do things according to my own desires rather than God's Divine Law. It's in these moments I envision God shaking His head and patiently sighing, "Really, Janet? I was hoping this time you would get it right. Try to do better next time, ok, for me?"

Journey to the Center of the World

It's fairly simple to determine if one is living in ego. Their statements and questions sound something like this: "What makes *me* happy?" "*I* want a divorce." "*I* should have gotten that promotion." "*I* deserve to have what *I* want." "*I* shouldn't have to wait." "Did you see what he just did to *me*?" I, I, I, *me*, *me*, *me* - it's all about the self. The world revolves around me. I am the center of the universe. I matter more than others. I concern myself first and foremost with my own personal interests. One who lives in Spirit queries, "Lord, what is it *you* want from me? How do *you* want me to respond to this person who insulted me? What are *your* plans for me? How do *you* want me to act in this situation? What pleases *you*? What is *your* will?" *You, you, you* - Spirit is all about God. I focus my actions on what is pleasing to Him and what aligns with His heart and mind.

When people learned I was writing a new book, they were curious as to what the subject matter was. I could only explain that it had to do with a radical shift in the way we live our lives, guaranteed to bring greater fulfillment and joy than ever imagined. Interestingly, about 90% guessed it was about pursuing what makes us happy - pure ego.

Who's the Turkey?

Yesterday was Thanksgiving. My husband has children from his first marriage as do I. His are scattered around the country and with them his adorable grandchildren. It is extremely rare when they all converge at the same time and in the same location. The past few years, this is exactly what has transpired on Thanksgiving, at his ex's house. The first year it occurred, we were invited to join them. I chose to spend it with my family as I had always done (as it turned out, it would be the last such holiday with my dad). I understood my husband choosing to be with his children (it was not about being with his ex – that I knew for sure).

The following year it occurred again. I said nothing. Then Easter – still I remained silent, followed by Lead East (the world's largest 50's party). I wasn't invited – it was supposed to be guy's night out, just him and his sons. Turns out, his ex joined them as well. It was beginning to feel uncomfortable for me. Fast forward to earlier this week - I approached him and asked if we would be together for Turkey Day or was he planning to go to his ex's? You guessed it. *Wrong answer*, I thought. I decided it was time to speak up.

I never tell my husband what he can and cannot do. He has always been free to decide for himself, as I believe marriage was intended to be. However, I did inform him I was not happy. "We're married and it's important to me that we are together for special occasions. If you want to spend a holiday with your children, you know they have always been invited to come here. I am not telling you what to do but I am telling you I am not happy about this." (Neither was he – he hates when I confront him about anything.)

For the next several days, I felt as if I was in a boxing ring, fighting an internal battle against myself. On the one hand, he's *my* husband. (Ooh, how possessive! But the label in his jeans says he belongs to me, doesn't it - right after the word *Levi*?) In my mind, it's inappropriate to be with her anymore (even though it was not about her – it was about his children). Ego wanted him to tell me he had reconsidered and was joining me at my sister's. Spirit presented a strong argument, "Why should you have it your way? He has just as much right to do what he wants as you do. Your desires do not carry greater importance than his, my dear." Ego was powerful and relentless and poor Spirit was taking a beating. I kept praying to God to change my heart. By round fifteen, Spirit, broken and bloody, was going down for the count. Seconds before the bell rung in defeat, Spirit sprung to her feet and with a blind upper-cut to the jaw, dropped Ego to the mat. Spirit raised her hands to the heavens and declared victory! In the eleventh hour, God worked His magic and changed my heart. I was at peace with my husband's choice. Later that day, as he put his coat on to leave, he gave me a kiss goodbye and apologized. "I'm sorry. Next year we'll work it out differently." (I wasn't looking for that anymore.)

That was a fast turn-around even for karma. While my motive was not for *him* to have a change of heart, God immediately blessed me for loving him enough to be completely ok with his decision. No good deed goes unrewarded.

Sin - Separated in Negativity

When I live in ego, I am easily misled by the temptations of the world. I become self-centered and selfish, making bad choices based on my own ignorance or the misguided intentions of others. Life is difficult and I am easily led down a path of self-destruction.

When ego consumes me, I err. This is what is commonly referred to as *sin*, a term in archery meaning to fall short of hitting the mark or the bull's-eye. I strive for virtue yet fall to imperfection, revealing my character defects and weaknesses.

However, when I reside in Spirit, I make righteous choices. All answers come from Divine Source. Any question asked is answered with Truth. Any decision made is based on a foundation of wisdom and Love. My direction leads me on a path of integrity and uprightness.

> *A Spirit-based life alleviates suffering while allowing for infinite joy and unlimited victory.*

I don't have all the answers - God does. I may think I know what is best for me - God knows for certain. Sometimes I love myself and do the right thing - God loves me constantly and always blesses me with what is in my best interest.

> *When I choose to follow His path and live a life that pleases Him, I receive abundant rewards and blessings.*

Until then, I, like the rest of this planet, will continue to struggle. God understands this, just as a teacher recognizes not every student is proficient in math. It takes some longer than others to learn. A great teacher consistently exhibits patience and guidance as long as the student demonstrates an interest. On the days the student fails to put forth a good effort, the teacher takes into consideration all extenuating circumstances - perhaps the child is ill, maybe there is something weighing heavily on his/her mind or perhaps they is distracted by something outside of their control. The teacher does not simply grade on outcome but equally on effort. So it is with the Great Teacher. His patience is unlimited - His guidance never ending.

> "Never will I leave you; never will I forsake you." So say with confidence, "The Lord is my helper; I will not be afraid."
> ~ Hebrews 13:5,6

Denial – Not Just a River in Egypt

As I mentioned earlier, we all live in denial. I began working with battered women at a homeless shelter back in the '90's. For the first time in my life I was exposed to a culture completely foreign to the one I was accustomed to. Violence, gossip, hate, and revenge contradicted the Christian values instilled in me by my parents - respect, kindness, forgiveness, and generosity, just to name a few. It was, to say the least, a rude awakening for me. These behaviors were a common thread among the majority of our residents. While many professed to be Christians, they clearly were not living the teachings of Christ. Some were proficient in quoting the Bible, "an eye for an eye" being among their favorites. However, like so many others, recitations from Scripture are often interpreted to suit their own personal needs and validate their offensive behaviors.

On one particular Monday evening during our anger management group, I posed the following question to my clients, "How would you describe yourself?" One resident responded, "I'm the nicest person you'd ever want to meet. I'd do anything for anyone." (*That's nice* *to hear,* I thought.) "Just don't ever cross me. I'll make your life hell. You'll regret the day you ever messed with me." Yikes! She can't be serious! Sad to say, she was – dead serious. And she was not alone. Several other women in the room chided in that they were the same, someone adding "and if I don't like you, you best leave me the f*alone." (Oh, Lord, what have I gotten myself into?)

Clearly these women are deceiving themselves that they are following the Word of God because as it states in the Bible, if someone takes your eye, take his as well, right? But doesn't God instruct us that if someone strikes you on one cheek to offer him the other and if someone takes your tunic give him your cloak as well? And of course, we're all familiar with "Vengeance is mine, says the Lord"?

> "You have heard that it was said, 'an eye for an eye and a tooth for tooth.' But I tell you not to resist an evil person. But whoever slaps you on your right cheek, turn the other to him also. If anyone wants to sue you and take away your tunic, let him have your cloak also." ~ Matthew 5:38 -40

Jesus is raising the standard of righteousness by asking us to extend grace to those who have offended us. In this way, we are given the opportunity to show them the merciful heart of our Lord.

Lessons in the Outfield

Forgiveness is discussed throughout the Bible and even appears in the Lord's Prayer - "Forgive us our trespasses as *we forgive those* who trespass against us".

Love does not seek revenge, ever. Love exemplifies a mélange of teaching and healing. If I seek vengeance on one who offends or cheats me, aren't I encouraging more of the same? How can I possibly teach anything other than that which I have just practiced? A hypocrite is one whose words and actions contradict one another. Both parties remain trapped in ignorance rather than undergo a spiritual transformation. Am I not ordained to be a *living example* of God's Word?

Imagine a child playing baseball - he stands in the outfield as his coach hits him a grounder. "Catch the ball!" the coach yells. The child stands with his glove outstretched in front of him as the ball passes through his legs. Does not a good coach approach him and show him the proper way to field a ground ball? Without judgment or condemnation, he places his gloved hand on the soil in the path of the ball, the other positioned as a backup. In that way, the child learns to become a skilled catcher. He and his coach celebrate a lesson well-learned and victory over ignorance. This is the way of Spirit. Had the coach chosen revenge and humiliated the child in front of his teammates by making an example of him, the child would have only learned shame, distrust, anger, and bitterness. Where is there glory in that?

Being punished and suffering for our mistakes does not please the Father. God wants us to learn in every situation and joyfully celebrates each subsequent victory with us. He is Teacher by example and we are called upon to embody His way in each of our relationships.

Buy American?

I am not one to engage in political or religious debates. Although they can lend themselves to a very spirited and educational dialogue, I find them too controversial. Too often people are not simply passionate about their beliefs and opinions but also intolerant of opposing views. What begins as an opportunity to share diverse opinions can easily erupt into a full-blown argument with hurt feelings and broken relationships.

Recently, though, I ignored my own rules and engaged in a somewhat political discussion. A family member broached the subject of automobiles and declared we should all *buy American*. I've driven Hondas for nearly 30 years. They suit my needs on a variety of levels. One member called me *un-American* (ouch!) because I was supporting the economy of a foreign country as opposed to my own. I confirmed that Honda is manufactured in Ohio but apparently that was of no significance. I continued to state that while I could certainly appreciate his perspective and belief, I didn't think God would object. He twisted and distorted his face as he uttered, "What does God have to do with it? That doesn't even make any sense!" he stated.

I explained, "God sees no geographical distinctions between nations or land masses. We are all His beloved children. He loves each of us as He loves the others, there is no dissimilarity. We are all brothers and sisters in one universal family, with God as our Heavenly Father. He wants prosperity equally for each of us. His mind does not think in terms of Americans vs. Chinese, Christians vs. Muslims or dark skinned vs. light skinned. I have two sons and two daughters. I would be appalled and deeply saddened if their attitude towards one another was boys against girls and vice versa. That way of thinking is understandable in children. But as adults we need to mature beyond our self-indulgent ways and align our minds with the mind of the Father. Remember, He is the Truth and the Way."

Reactions were mixed. Some huffed and puffed and dismissed my beliefs as ridiculous, others paused in contemplation, and one appeared to find validity in my principles but seemed reluctant to acquiesce. No matter. I stated how I felt. I am not here to convince. My objective was simply to provide others with something new to consider and to engage them in thinking in new directions. When I discover something that transforms my life I feel a moral obligation to offer it to others. What they do with it once it is presented to them is entirely between them and God.

Inquiring Minds Need to Know

I abhor gossip. Speaking poorly about others never sat well with me. I despise tabloids that feed off the

> "I, the LORD, speak the truth, I declare what is right."
> ~ Isaiah 45:19

suffering of celebrities while deliberately creating untruths about them. Politicians campaigning for office spend more

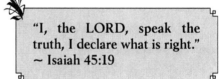

> "They have become filled with every kind of wickedness, evil, greed, and depravity. They are full of envy, murder, strife, deceit, and malice. They are gossips." ~ Romans 1:29

time debasing their opponent than touting their own qualifications and accomplishments. Divorced couples despicably demean their child's other

parent and engage in parental alienation. In each of these cases, the culprit pathetically tries to justify their actions, oftentimes claiming

> "These are the things you are to do - speak the truth to each other and render true and sound judgment in your courts." ~ Zechariah 8:16

they must be *purveyors of truth*. After all, inquiring minds have a right to know, right? And who better to bring truth to the forefront than one who has no preceding agenda with their competition nor stands to gain financially from their actions? What they declared as truth is more often than not opinion and very often outright lies. What is their motive for relaying such personal or unflattering information, whether factual or not?

A gossiper's behavior reveals more about their own lack of integrity than it does about the other's (alleged) indiscretions.

~

Joey Shoemaker

No where in the Bible is there reference to God deliberately or inadvertently spreading false information about any of His children in a desperate attempt to defame someone, cause a rift between friends or family or to promote popularity and financial gain for Himself. Could you imagine Jesus preaching the Word of God while slandering the name of those committing sins against His Father?

> *"Hey, Pete. Did you hear that Joe the shoemaker is having an affair with his wife's sister? True, dude! I saw it for myself! Can you believe it? I've never really liked him. And there was this other guy, you know, the tax collector – well, I heard he was taking bribes and skimming money off the top for himself. How else could he have afforded to buy two new donkeys? He couldn't do that on his salary alone."*

How ludicrous does that sound? And yet we do it every day and actually think we sound intelligent. And worse yet, we fail to see the malice behind our words. This is the perfect time for a reality check. Stand before a mirror and with brutal honesty, ask yourself, "If God were standing before me, what would He say to me?" (FYI - He is.) Then ask if your behavior pleases Him. Surprised?

When I act in a just and fair manner, I am at one with Divine Love.

> *When my mind and actions are void of prejudice, bias, favoritism, and malice, Father is pleased and abundant blessings follow.*

When my heart is filled with love I seek to enrich the lives of all whom I meet. I actively live and uphold equality for all my brothers and sisters. I declare myself color-blind and see beyond outward appearances. I remove all desire to see others suffer and *get what's coming to them.* I diligently avoid causing harm to all living creatures. I love freely, unconditionally, and without limitations and conditions. Then and only then have I mastered the mind of the Master.

You're *How* Old?

Two of my clients (a couple) are facing divorce. The husband, recognizing he failed in some aspects of his relationship, sought to make amends. Sitting in my office, he professed his love for his wife and the deep remorse he felt for having neglected her. She agreed to try and make their marriage work. However, she could not move beyond the past and repeatedly reminded him of the offenses he committed. His patience wore thin. Eventually he lashed back. "I'm not the only one who made mistakes! You hurt me, too," he shouted. "But you did it first!" She lashed back. (Oh, Lord! Are these two even old enough to be married? They were nearing retirement age so my guess was, chronologically, they were.) Flabbergasted, I asked, "Really? You've got to be kidding!" My response caught both of them off-guard. "Have you listened to yourselves? Do you think you even remotely sound like adults?"

Both were clearly stuck in ego and wallowing in self-pity. The husband initiated in Spirit but was subsequently engulfed in the quicksand of self-righteousness. A disconnect from Divine triggers remarks based on fear, pain, self-preservation, and so forth. Spirit is sensitive to the other's feelings and needs, cares about their best interest, and implores God to lovingly form the words they are about to express. Spirit instinctively knows that whatever the outcome God will make matters right for each party even if it does not conform to their own vision. My reaction to, and treatment of, another is a matter between me and God.

Grandmas and Grandkids and Games - Oh My!

I had been estranged from several of my children for many years. When I had last seen my oldest grandson he was nine months of age. When he re-entered my life he was six and a half. Seeing him for the first time in more than five years, I remember thinking to myself, *he doesn't know who I am. He has so many other grandparents who have been there from the get-go. What would make him care about me?* Grandparents often want to be the favorite of sorts - the fun grandma, the one who creates fond childhood memories, and makes the child feel special. I knew I didn't want to get caught up in a *me* mindset. It was childish and immature and I was setting myself up to be hurt if, in fact, he loved the others more than me. I prayed to God and immediately felt my heart open. *"Allow him to love as he chooses. He knows who you are. Let the relationship flow naturally to where it is meant to be, not where you want it to go."* I chose to be grateful I was given the opportunity to know him. I felt at peace as I allowed the relationship to unfold unpretentiously.

> **My way leads to disappointment and pain.**
> **God's way abolishes suffering by restoring**
> **gratitude and serenity.**

Today, ours is a very loving and special relationship.

The competition that exists within families is fierce, causing significant dissention and feuds, tearing families apart, and leaving broken relationships strewn like worthless trash along the roadway. Do you think for even one fraction of a moment that it pleases God to see His family shattered into tiny fragments of wounded hearts? Dick and Tom Smothers (of Smothers Brothers fame) were two of my favorite comedians back in the '60's. Tommy Smothers' most infamous line to his brother was "Mom always liked you best." In a comedic skit, this is entertaining and amusing. But it real life, it can easily lead to low self-esteem, jealousy, anger, fighting, and family rifts. Do you think this is what God had in mind when He created family, a select unit of His children brought together to live, love, nurture, and enjoy one another? Spirit allows for love to flow effortlessly exactly where it is needed most - exactly to where God appoints it.

Forty Good Years

For the first forty-some years of my life, my family escaped the trivial nonsense so many others struggled with, for which I am deeply grateful. However, issues of perceived favoritism and jealousy gradually emerged, forming deep gauges in once tight and loving bonds. While I am powerless to heal those rifts, my concern first and foremost is to behave in a manner pleasing to my Lord. Have I carefully and honestly examined my role in these issues? Have I openly admitted to my transgressions or insensitivities? Have I reached out in love and concern to make amends? If I have sincerely acted in a manner consistent with the mind and Commandments of God, I can be at peace with myself and seek to uncover what God wants me to do next.

Revenge is a gravely destructive force and an abomination against God.

Scripture states,

> "Vengeance is mine, I will repay', says the Lord." ~ Romans 12: 19-21

Before some of you begin gloating, "God will get 'em and make them pay!", let me explain. At first glance, it may seem as though God will impose punishment on sinners for their wrongdoings. But He is not a God of retribution. He is one of healing. He further instructs us...

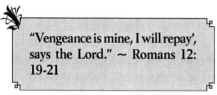

> "If your enemy is hungry, feed him, if he is thirsty give him something to drink... Do not be overcome by evil but overcome evil with good." ~ Romans 12:20

"*Overcome evil with good*" - seriously, Lord? Isn't it enough I don't punch him in the face for what he did? Now you want me to feed him and give him something to quench his thirst? *Exactly!* In this way, not only do I exemplify Truth but...

> *I protect myself from being defeated by sin and I am transformed by kindness and rewarded with God's favor.*

Additionally, I have set the example for the offending party to learn and come to know the Way, similar to the coach and his catcher in the previous text.

According to Dr. Wayne Dyer, research shows that a simple act of kindness improves the immune system and increases the production of serotonin in all parties - the one receiving the kindness as well as the giver. Kindness, whether offered, received or even witnessed, benefits the physical and emotional health of all involved. From a purely health perspective, refraining from retribution and acting instead on kindness reaps significant benefits.

Remember, too, only God understands what is in the heart and mind of each of us - what issues we are struggling with and what our motivations are. I must have faith enough in God and trust that He can and does care for each of us, sans punishment. I need not overstep His authority. My role is always to work on myself. I am to love others as God loves and whenever possible, show them the path to the Kingdom of God by my example. Everything else belongs to Father.

Love Your Enemies and Set Boundaries

"Ok, but what about those times people put me at risk - someone who is physically harming me or stealing from me? Do I just smile politely and tell them I love them, because that's just not going to happen!" I hear you. And no, God does not want or expect us to allow others to deliberately hurt us, use us or cause us unnecessary hardship. In my previous book, <u>The Secret Side of Anger</u>, I devote an entire chapter to the subject of setting and enforcing boundaries in relationships. We have a God-given right to be treated with dignity and respect at all times. If a person is causing us harm, either physically, emotionally, sexually, mentally, financially or in any other form, we must put a stop to it.

> "Thou shalt love thy neighbor as thyself." ~ Leviticus 19:18

We are instructed to love ourselves *enough* so as not to allow others to mistreat us in any way, shape or form. Just as God expects us to treat others with kindness, He requires that we ensure others treat us likewise. In situations such as these, we need to set and enforce strict boundaries to safeguard our well-being.

> "This is what the Lord Almighty says, 'Administer true justice, show mercy and compassion to one another.'" ~ Zechariah 7:9

CHAPTER 5

(Not) David Letterman's Top Ten

Yakity Yak – Don't Talk Back

People speak at the Father all the time. I deliberately chose the word *at* because our conversations are usually very one-sided. Many ask favors of Him - "Lord, help me get this promotion." "Please keep my children safe." "Let all of my lab tests come back negative." Still others pose questions - "Should I tell my brother off or just let this issue slide?" "Am I the one with the problem or is the rest of the world screwed up?" (The answer is "yes", by-the-way, to that last question.) "What am I supposed to do now that my children have all grown up and moved out?" In some ways, these questions are rhetorical - we don't really expect an answer or at least not in the first person.

And while many speak, few literally hear a response. I converse with the Father daily. Most of the time, I don't hear a reply as I would when I speak with, let's say, my mom. Most often, there is silence (reminiscent of when I'm speaking with my husband). I'm never quite sure if I'm simply not paying attention or God hasn't given me His reply yet. There are moments, too, when He clearly responds but I brush Him off. It isn't the answer I wanted so I dismiss it, hoping for a better one. (I'm very patient, God. I can wait all night if I have to.)

How can I ever be 100% certain that the answer to **"Does This Please God?"** is the right one? Unless the Lord gives me two thumbs up, won't there be some doubt? Most probably, there will be. While some questions will be answered with crystal clarity, others, quite frankly, will not. Don't worry about this. What matters most to God is not exclusively our actions but equally, if not more importantly, our intentions and effort.

I spent fifteen years struggling with an eating disorder (bulimia). It was a living hell. The uncontrollable cycle of bingeing and purging plunged me into vortex of despair. Shame and self-deprecation kept the disorder hidden from family and friends for many years as I spiraled deeper and deeper into desolation. Overwhelming feelings of hopelessness and powerlessness left me feeling completely disconnected from God. In my shame, I couldn't face Him. I imagined His disappointment in me. "You're stronger than that, Janet." And the anger! "I gave you a healthy body and you're destroying it! How ungrateful can you be?" The sight of my own reflection in the mirror disgusted me.

Teflon Shoes On Ice

I struggled so hard for what seemed to be an eternity. Enrolling in a support group, enlisting the aid of a licensed therapist, and attempting behavior modification techniques – I tried it all. But it was akin to walking up an icy hill wearing Teflon shoes - I couldn't gain any traction.

The battle was exhausting as I kept sliding downhill. The more I digressed, the less mental and physical energy I had to continue.

I have to admit there were times when I didn't want to relinquish it. After all, it served a purpose - food was comforting. Growing up in a big Italian family, food was the answer to everything. When you're tired – mangia, if you're sick – mangia, and when you're sad or celebrating - mangia! Eat! Eat! When my marriage failed, food was a logical choice to soothe my broken heart. It felt like love and filled a massive void in my life. But it had another purpose as well - being a single mom raising four children on my own and running a business was a daunting challenge. Managing my weight was something I did not want to think about, much less put effort into. It afforded me the luxury (or so I thought) of being able to eat whatever I wanted and not worry about gaining weight. I wasn't concerned with how it was destroying my life from the inside out.

I was an addict. Rationalizing that at least I was not using an illegal substance offered little comfort. I fluctuated between desperate resignation of my sentence to glaring determination for liberation.

Platinum Spatula Award

All the while, I believe God credited me for my efforts (when I made them). He saw me try. He knew the depth and nature of my suffering that precipitated this disorder and knew there were going to be obstacles to my success, many of which had to do with issues of dangerously low self-esteem and years of repressed emotions. He also knew I could not overcome those barriers until I was ready. He is a God of great patience and compassion. While I am certain He was not elated with my self-destructive behavior, He fully appreciated every effort I put into my recovery.

I am reminded of a time many decades ago when my children were young. It was Mother's Day and like many young children, they wanted to do something special for me. Take a guess - breakfast (thankfully, not in bed) - eggs, toast, and juice. They were so cute! Just thinking about it brings a smile to my face. The eggs were runny (*that* does not bring back fond memories), the toast a bit charred (the burnt you can scrape off), but the oj was perfect! While their culinary skills would not secure them a place on the next Food Network Star Challenge, their efforts scored them the Platinum Spatula Award. (I just made that up.) Like any mother, I deeply appreciated their efforts and bestowed upon them well-deserved praise.

Good Things Come in Ten's

The human body is quite a remarkable and complex organ, perfectly designed and executed, enabling us to accomplish amazing feats. If given the original task of creating the first human prototype, would you or I have chosen to give it ten fingers and ten toes? Why ten, why not four or seven? For whatever the reason, God chose a perfect ten. Imagine how much more challenging it would be to complete a task with only five or three? Sure, humans are resourceful and more than likely would have figured something out. But isn't life so much easier with ten fully-functioning fingers? And imagine trying to walk or run or balance on less than ten toes? It's the perfect number necessary to make mobility effortless. (And it's the ideal number of perfectly painted toenails needed to look stunning in a pair of strappy summer sandals. Right, ladies?) My point (which I'll eventually get around to making) is this - God deliberately chose this number.

I cannot imagine any of us intentionally choosing to discard or ignore any of the ten appendages of our extremities stating some are unnecessary, were not designed realistically ("the thumb is too fat and the pinky toe too short) while others are completely outdated. That would be ludicrous, wouldn't it? Yet, that is the very same reasoning some apply to God's ten perfect laws of life (the Commandments) - they're outdated, unrealistic, and impractical in today's world. But how can that be? That would mean God, as we know Him, is fallible and makes mistakes. Not my God – He is the absolute and complete source of all knowledge.

Asking "**Does This Please God?**" is not a question one must answer by themselves. God has already given us the tools with which to do so. The answers are clearly outlined in...

God's Top Ten

In Exodus 24, God said to Moses,

> "Come up to Me, to the mountain, and remain there. I will give you the stone tablets, the commandment that I have written for the people's instruction." ~ Exodus 24:12

The Ten Commandments

1. I, the Lord, am your God. You shall not have other gods besides me.
2. You shall not take the name of the Lord God in vain.
3. Remember to keep holy the Lord's Day.
4. Honor your father and your mother.
5. You shall not kill.
6. You shall not commit adultery.
7. You shall not steal.

8. You shall not bear false witness.
9. You shall not covet your neighbor's wife.
10. You shall not covet your neighbor's goods.

Take note that these are *commandments*, not *suggestions*. A command is a rule of authority, a mandate from the one in power. God is *instructing* us to follow His Divine Law and promises if we do, our lives will be fruitful and rewarding.

Have you ever purchased a piece of furniture or a bike for your child? They come with *instructions*, not recommendations. They convey with assuredness that for your own safety and protection, and to guarantee you derive the most enjoyment and benefits from their product, you *must follow* their directives in *precise detail*. Failure to do so could result in serious injury or death and invalidates product warranty. The manufacturer is not liable for injury or compensation under these circumstances. Failure to follow God's instructions implicitly can lead to serious injury or death. However, He offers an eternal warranty.

The Big Scream Assembly

Reading instructions has never been my forte but when my son was little, I purchased a bike for him called the Big Green Scream Machine. Typically, I would leave the assembly for my husband. However, he was away on business and Chris couldn't wait to ride his new big wheel. So I opened the box, took out the instructions and fainted (kidding!). After calming down and reminding myself that a million other people had already assembled this product, I proceeded to lay out the pieces (including all the nuts and bolts) in the identical pattern as the illustration depicted. With the appropriate tools, one-by-one I inserted each screw into the proper cutout and connected the correct pieces in sequence. After several stressful hours, I rose from the basement floor proclaiming victory over the intimidating lime-colored sidewalk cycle! I learned a valuable lesson that day - things work so much better and last longer when one chooses to follow the manufacturer's directive. And the ride is way more fun!

Knowing this, why do we so vigorously resist God's instructions? Perhaps in part it is due to arrogance. "I'm an adult. I can make my own decisions. I don't need anyone telling me what to do." We seem to think being an adult is equivalent to being infallible. And some, though recognizing their limitations, are fully willing to take responsibility for bad choices and the consequences that follow. "So what if I mess up - it's my problem." But do we take into account the many innocent people who will also suffer as a result of the other's bad judgment? For example - an individual chooses to drink and get behind the wheel of a car ("If kill myself, oh well!"). There are few who would support their reasoning knowing the devastation that can occur should they cause an accident. And there is always a possibility an innocent bystander will lose their life due to his or her inebriation, leaving behind families consumed with grief.

I've always respected the Ten Commandments and have made a sincere effort to live each one, although those who know me well will eagerly attest to my miserable failures. One afternoon, while discussing them with my mom (the Commandments, not my pathetic fiascos), I mentioned I found them to be somewhat simplistic. They were, in my opinion, lacking some necessary components to cover all of life's temptations and issues. Being well-versed in Biblical studies, Mom informed me that while they may appear to be one-dimensional they go into much greater detail than one would imagine.

Commandment 1

"I, the Lord, am your God. You shall not put other gods before me."

That's pretty straight forward, don't you think? Believe in and worship only the One True God. "I do that so I'm off to a good start!" Yet, how often do we put other people or things before our love of God? It is easy to see how misguided society has become in whom and what they worship. Some put money before God - rather than spending time in Sunday worship, they're hustling to earn more cash. (Let me clarify - I am not referring to those who are legitimately struggling just to make ends meet. There are considerations in every case.) For those who have acquired much it is easy to become greedy, wanting even more financial wealth.

I have seen men worship women and women who need to be adored and glorified by their peers. (Remember Charlie Sheen and his infamous *goddesses*?) People have been consumed with power and control and place their status far above that of God's. Others have exalted material possessions, never finding satisfaction with what they already have. (How many pairs of shoes does one realistically need?) Some put their love of food or drugs or alcohol or sex above the Almighty, and there are still others who deify themselves as the center of the universe - the egotistical, narcissistic, proud, arrogant, and the self-righteous.

While these behaviors and attitudes are easy to see in others, like everything else, we are reluctant to recognize them in ourselves. How disrespectful to God when we choose to live this way. Any violation of this commandment dishonors the Most High.

Commandment 2

"You shall not take the name of the Lord God in vain."

Where do I even begin? It has become increasingly more difficult to have a conversation with someone without hearing a "G** damn it" or "Jesus f***ing Christ" thrown around as freely as a morning salutation. To include the name of the Most High with profanity doesn't even make sense, let alone being highly offensive. Who among us would not take issue with someone inserting a curse word between their first and last name when they became angry? "Janet f***ing Pfeiffer!" I find that truly repugnant. And not only that, but I would never use profanity along with the name of someone I loved – my children, parents, friends or husband - not even my dogs! I can't imagine anyone being ok with that. And yet, it is deemed socially acceptable in God's case.

I must admit I used to say "G** damn it" when I was younger. Early on I realized I hated the way it sounded. Not only did it make me sound ignorant and crude, I didn't want to disrespect the Father I so deeply loved and appreciated. But old habits die hard. I began paying close attention to the words about to depart from my mouth before actually releasing them. I would catch myself at the first sound of "Guh" and slowed down the progression of my declaration to reconsider what I could use to replace the vulgarity. "Guh" turned into "good…morning…sunshine" in a very deliberate and conscious process. A declaration of "Jesus Christ" when I was angry (I never used a profane insert) was replaced with "Jeeze Louise!" using the same method. Even the expression "oh s**t" was modified to become "oh shitake mushrooms!" It's not difficult. It simply takes awareness, determination, and practice. And the desire to please God makes the process effortless - most of the time.

Commandment 3

"Remember to keep holy the Lord's Day."

I was raised with the belief that Sunday is the Lord's Day. It is the day Christians attend church to worship and praise the Lord followed by Sunday school to study the Bible. Chores were done on Saturdays. Stores opened Monday through Saturday were closed on the seventh, allowing families time to spend together. Perhaps, too, it was a time meant to contemplate the wonders of God without the distractions of our day-to-day responsibilities, to remember all we had to be thankful for, and to seek ways in which we could deepen our relationship with Him.

In the immature ways of a child, reserving only Sundays to be holy seemed silly. Did that mean the other six days a week it was ok to sin? (*If you're going to misbehave or commit a crime, just don't do it on the Lord's Day.*) That didn't make sense to me. But as I grew and matured, I understood this Commandment in another way - God created all seven days and each belongs to Him. Perhaps He expects us to be holy on every one. *Bergen County - Blue Laws*

Commandment 4

"Honor your father and mother."

I grew up in a generation that valued family. We held our parents and elders in high regard. Though not perfect, if nothing else, we respected their position of authority and responsibility for our care. I was blessed. I grew up with two of the best parents the world has ever known so it was easy to honor them. It was, at times, hard to follow their *outdated* rules yet I always respected them. There was never any back-talk or sassing. Neither my sisters nor I ever yelled at, cursed, threatened or disrespected either of them. And their treatment of us was mutual.

Not all children are as fortunate as my sisters and I. How can one follow this Commandment when the parents they were given were either absent, selfish, addicts, liars, criminals, abusers or worse? How does one respect and revere toxic parents?

To honor means *to respect* and respect is defined as *to value*. Children are expected to value their parents. And really, how is that any different from any other relationship? After all, we are all God's children regardless of the role we are currently assigned. Since none of us has more value in God's eyes than the other, isn't it logical we treat our parents with the same regard afforded others, even when they are less than perfect in their role?

Let me clarify - if a child is being beaten, verbally abused (or worse), neglected or placed in harm's way, they are not obligated to remain in close proximity with the insidious parent. It may be necessary to remove the child to a safer more nurturing environment. Yet that does not relieve them of their responsibility to hold their parents in high regard, at the very least, *as a child of God and the ones who brought them into this world*. They may not be eligible for the parent-of- the-year award but we must always love them in our hearts, forgive them for the mistakes they've made, and, whenever possible, be a part of their life in some capacity. After all, aren't we all acting out our pain on others? (Not acceptable, mind you - just understandable.)

Commandment 5

"You shall not kill."

You shall not kill, period, end of sentence. There is no *with the exception of* list I am aware of. Killing is killing. To take someone's life, a life that belongs exclusively to the Creator of All, is an abomination. Even against those who brutally ended the life of the Father's only Son, God chose not to seek revenge by executing those responsible. He set the ultimate example for us to follow.

There are many who believe in capital punishment. But what good does it accomplish to end someone's life because they are responsible for the death of another? When someone's life is taken in retribution, it does not restore life to the deceased. It has tragically produced two families who must navigate the grief process and attempt to restore their broken lives. And who am I to say when it is time for an individual to transition from this life? What if God has further plans for him or her that have not yet been realized? I have no right to interfere with His Divine Plan for any of His children. Capital punishment, abortion and war - all are an offense against the Creator of the Universe.

Killing is not exclusive to our physical bodies, either. How often are we responsible for destroying another's self-esteem through constant criticism or poisoning their dreams with negative remarks? We kill a person's reputation with idle gossip and crush their joy with disparaging remarks. We ruin their opportunities with our own selfish greed. We are reckless with the lives of others rather than holding them tenderly in our hearts, treating each as the sacred gift it is.

Commandment 6

"You shall not commit adultery."

"I've never cheated on anyone in my life so I'm good on this one. Moving right along..." Hold on. I've never cheated either but adultery is not limited to having an affair with someone who's married or to cheating on your current partner. Adultery is also defined as disloyal, false, betrayal, and deceitful. Hmm, perhaps we need to rethink our innocence regarding the Sixth Commandment.

Have you ever deceived someone into thinking you were someone or something other than who/what you really are? People often refer to me as their counselor or therapist. I remind them to be either one must be credentialed, which I am not. They may refer to me as their coach, mentor or guide (or their most favorite person ever in the whole world) but neither of the previous titles is appropriate. In no way do I ever want to mislead anyone. In fact, with my private clients, I have them sign a disclaimer stating they are fully aware of this fact.

Well, sure, professionally one must take strict precautions not to jeopardize the integrity of their business but what about in our personal lives? Have we ever pretended to be something other than who we really are?

In front of our families and friends we are warm and loving. Yet behind closed doors we spread vicious rumors and falsehoods about our cousin who allegedly cheated on his college boards. We berate our spouses in the privacy of our bedrooms while projecting the image of being a devoted partner. A friend shares a confidence and we ruthlessly furnish the information to others after a falling out.

We all know someone who drives an expensive Mercedes, wears Prada shoes, and carries Gucci handbags. They deceitfully depict themselves as being financially secure and wealthy when in fact they have maxed out their credit cards while living rent free with their 80-year-old mother. Talk shows are booked with guests ready to reveal a dark secret to their spouse, parent or friend. "I've gambled away our retirement fund," one tearful wife shamefully admitted in front of millions of viewers to her husband of forty-plus years.

When I was in college, I worked for a generous and personable business man. His employees were afforded an unprecedented company discount of 50% off any store merchandise. Everyone who knew him loved and admired him, except, that is, his creditors that held his loans. Investigation found he had a history of accruing large debts, only to file Chapter 11 time-and-time again. He was deceitful for sure, bilking unsuspecting investors out of their due. Scam artist – absolutely! Adulterer? You decide.

I am reminded of my childhood - I had a group of friends who were somewhat popular though certainly not the *in* crowd. We swore a loyalty to one another forever (as much as forever can apply to a twelve-year-old). But it wasn't long before one of our members dumped us for someone better. Well, *better* is subjective. Even though we were only in sixth grade, her disloyalty hurt. I never forgot that. It was a painful lesson that prevented me (I hope) from ever treating anyone in my life so poorly.

Do false or broken promises fall within the parameters of the Sixth Law of God? A local businessman in the town where I currently live promised if he ever sold his business, he would give the first option to buy to his store manager. Imagine the hurt when he abruptly sold it to a complete stranger without informing his loyal employee of the transaction?

Have you ever subscribed to internet dating sites? Talk about deception! We've all heard singles complain that the photos are not representative of what the person really looks like - someone who describes themselves as *tall* is actually 5'4" and hasn't weighed any where near 120 lbs since high school. Still others pledge their loyalty - "I promise if you lend me the money I'll pay you right back," only to betray their trust by defaulting on their debt.

And then of course, we have that ever present self-deceit - "I'm not sick. I know I've been coughing for two years but it's just an allergy. These cigarettes don't bother me at all." "I'm not an addict. I can quit drinking whenever I want to. I just don't want to right now." "I'm not saying this to hurt your feelings but ____. It's only because I care." (Care less, thank you very much.)

Still think the Sixth Commandment doesn't apply? Quite an eye opener, isn't it? It was for me, too. No judgment. Let's both just try harder.

Commandment 7

"You shall not steal."

Once again, many of you are probably thinking, *I don't go into stores and take things I haven't paid for so I can skip this*. And once again, I'm going to challenge you to rethink your position. (Not whether you're standing or sitting - not *that* position, silly!) I'm sure some of you may be getting discouraged but my role is not to make this easy for you. I'm here to help you face some difficult or unpleasant truths. Trust me - even with all the work I've done on myself, I'm doing this right along with you. The only way to God is to be a fearless seeker-of-truth and we are seeking truth, are we not?

Stealing involves far more than taking possessions that do not belong to us. We steal the hopes and dreams of others. How many parents have told their children not to try out for the school play because they're not talented? I remember as a child having an adult tell me not to bother going to college because I'd never amount to anything. Even though I was an honor-roll student and never got into trouble, this adult squashed any hopes I may have had of obtaining a college degree and subsequent career. Fortunately for me, my mom insisted I attend college even though in my heart I had no aspirations. That insidious thief robbed me of the ambition necessary for professional success early in my adult life. Thankfully, I was able to retrieve and recreate those desires upon reaching mid-life but not all are as fortunate as I.

Or consider your sister-in-law who is in a really good mood and you sabotage it by giving her startling statistics she simply *must* be made aware of at that precise moment. "I am so happy today! It's our fifth wedding anniversary and I'm married to the most wonderful man in the world." In that specific moment, you feel compelled to inform her about a recent study just released revealing 72% of all married men cheat on their wives within the first five years of marriage. (I made up those stats to prove a point. I'm certain more than 18% of you guys have more integrity than that.) You have sucked the joy right out of her and, unless she is consciously aware and able to prevent it, you just ruined her day.

And what about the notepads, paperclips, and pens you bring home from work? They don't really count, do they? After all, the company you work for is a Fortune 500 and the CEO's have enormous expense accounts. You know for a fact, many are extorting funds from the company on a regular basis. So what's a few notepads? Anyhow, you deserve them. You work hard, put in long hours, and bring home a paycheck a mouse couldn't survive on. Besides, you've seen them throw away more supplies than what you're taking. So, this is one instance where "you shall not steal" doesn't apply, right? (Hmm.)

Have you ever cheated on your income tax return, filed a false insurance claim or exaggerated about injuries sustained in a work-related incident? Have you taken credit for someone else's ideas or convinced someone to terminate their friendship with another in order to be friends with you? Have you borrowed money, a dress or a shovel from a neighbor and conveniently forgotten to return it? Writers plagiarize other author's materials. People have their identities stolen. Individuals find a lost item and fail to search for or return it to its rightful owner. (The *finder's keepers* rule is not exempt from this Commandment, by the way.)

The laundry list goes on and on. We cannot minimize or justify taking that which is not ours simply by using the lame excuse, "Well, everyone does it." Everyone speeds, too, but it's still breaking the law and putting others at risk. And when I get caught, I'm going to get ticketed. Remember, God sees every infraction.

Commandment 8

"You Shall Not Bear False Witness."

I have gorgeous black bears that pass through my yard and they are in no way false. Believe me, they are *very* real! Oh… not those kinds of bears? Mea culpa.

Exactly what does it mean to bear false witness? One of the foremost examples that come to mind is rumors and gossip. It's a hot topic I speak passionately about in high schools as well as at the battered women's shelter. We are all familiar with the gossip mongers in our lives - the coworker who knows all the latest goings-on of everyone in the building and shares even the most personal information freely and without reservation.

We've witnessed the spiteful son who received less than his share of the inheritance who suddenly reveals the *special* relationship his parents had with the other sibling. Or consider the neighbor who watches people come and go all hours of the day and night, then shares the local gossip with township reporters. And of course there's the divorced wife who dishes all the dirt of her husband's, let's say, *less than stellar* performance in the boudoir or the second place winner of a prestigious sporting event accusing the winner of cheating.

"I really hate people like that. I would never gossip! I couldn't care less what other people are doing. I mind my own business." Really? Because even I gossip. I'm not proud of it but I am being truthful. I do talk about people behind their backs. But of course, you see, for me it's because I care about them. Well, that's what I sometimes deceive myself into believing and that's what I would like you to believe about me as well. But truth be told, there are times when my motives are less than pure. I try to be aware of the times when speaking poorly about another is actually an attempt to raise my value in my own eyes and (hopefully) in the other's. "My husband spends money on the most frivolous items. I do without and scrimp and save to balance the budget each month." Doesn't that make him look bad to others when in reality my closets are not starving for garments? In fact, there are clothes from years ago still wearing the original price tags. "That's only because I need two complete four-season wardrobes - one for casual and one for business," I try to rationalize. Because I'm so frugal in most areas, I have difficulty seeing my somewhat extravagant spending habits in others. Yet it's blatantly apparent to me as I put my husband under a microscope. A reality check of my motives for speaking poorly about a wonderful husband is very much in order.

As I stand in line each week at the local Shoprite, I see empty display racks where current issues of the tabloids no longer dwell. Are you one of the millions who support their sales and voluntarily share the latest celebrity dirt with others you know? It's not like you're doing anything wrong, though. After all, you didn't make this stuff up. It's already public knowledge. You're simply discussing the latest in current events. And besides, it's not like you actually know these stars. And let's not forget, when you become famous you give up the right to your privacy. (Sigh.)

The Blame Game

The purpose of gossip and rumors is to harm the targeted party, to damage their reputation or to cause injury or hardship to them. Does anyone for a moment believe this is ok with God? I don't think He likes excuses. Or blame – He's not particularly fond of blame either. We often falsely accuse others of our own wrongdoings. When my children were in high school, it was only a few short days before Christmas and like most mothers, I was rushing around trying to accomplish the impossible. I was stressed to my breaking point. My oldest daughter wanted to go shopping with some of her friends at a local mall. "Mom, can you drop me off and pick me up later?" I had already told her I would be baking cookies all day and could not accommodate her request. So, she asked the mother of one of her friends to drive her. "Are you sure you'll have a ride home?" I asked. She assured me she would. Guess where I'm going with this. That's right - around 4:30 that afternoon, the phone rang. "Mom", I heard her voice. "Say no more", I instructed her. "You need a ride, right?" I was furious! I pulled the tray of candy cane cookies out of the oven and turned the dial to *off*. I wasted no time getting to the mall. (That's an indirect way of saying I was driving somewhat faster than the law allowed. Ok, I was speeding... a little. Agh! No excuses, Janet!)

I've shopped at this mall a thousand times and am fully aware of the *no left turn* sign as I entered from Berdan Ave. This time, it didn't quite register as I flipped on my directional. Too late – a car approaching from the other direction slammed into the passenger side of my vehicle. The crunching sound of metal made me painfully aware of the accident I just caused. That's right, it was my fault and I openly admitted it, to the other driver as well. The *never admit fault* mindset contradicts this Commandment. I could have blamed it on someone else - my daughter for making me pick her up when I clearly told her I was not able to, the other driver for not seeing me (it was a blind spot – hence the *no left turn* sign - duh!), retailers for putting people under abnormal amounts of pressure around the holidays, blah, blah, blah. But the reality was there was no one to blame but yours truly. I made a bad choice and I needed to own up to my mistake and not divert it to another. "Bear false witness" - nope, not even an option.

We all try to blame others for what's not working in our lives. "It's not my fault" and "I can't help it" are frequent excuses (and they *are* excuses) we've all used, some more than others. That confirms that our miserable lives, failures, and mistakes are actually the responsibility of someone else which, in essence, means I have no ownership in my own life. Now there's a scary thought! When we speak untruths (lies and deceptions), or fail to articulate the truth, we damage reputations, cause hardship, suffering, hurt, and sometimes destroy lives.

Soon after the Casey Anthony verdict (a case where a young mother was accused of being responsible for the death of her two-year-old daughter), her parents were interviewed on the Dr. Phil Show. I watched snippets of his two-part broadcast with great interest. It was evident to me her parents knew more than they had revealed in court. In an attempt to protect their daughter from the consequences of this tragic loss, they may have conveyed false information against one another. After all, if Casey was innocent then someone else was guilty, at the very least, of negligence. To lie to cover up for a culpable party, even if it be our child, lends suspicion to an innocent person.

While out with friends one afternoon, someone posed the question, "If your child committed a horrible crime, let's say murder, would you lie to protect them?" Without hesitation, several parents responded with a resounding "Of course!" I felt torn. As a mother, yes, I would undoubtedly lie. Yet as a Christian, it would violate my commitment to God's Eighth Law. I realized I am currently unable to answer that question with certainty and I could never fully know unless put in that situation.

"False witness" - incorrect, dishonest, misleading, and deceitful - all contradict the very nature of Truth.

Stop!

Commandment 9

10/24/19

"You Shall Not Covet Your Neighbor's Wife"

(FYI, this Commandment appears to be addressing men but is inclusive of both genders.)

When I was a little girl and first learned about the Commandments in Sunday school, I thought God was speaking about *covering* your neighbor's wife. I imagined someone putting a bedspread over the lady next door and wondering why it was wrong. *If she's hiding under a blanket no one will be able to find her.* That seemed strange. My adult mind has a much clearer understanding of what it means to covet - to be envious of and to desire. Infidelity is as old as time. People seek the company of another's spouse, disregarding the sacred vows the couple made when entering into this holy union - to love, honor, cherish, and *be faithful to* till death.

> "Marriage should be honored by all and the marriage bed kept pure..." ~ Hebrews 13:4-7

Many do not respect the sanctity of marriage. The Bible tells us marriage is a sacred union between a man and a woman created by God the Almighty.

Many men and women admit to having affairs (*admit to*, that's not the number

> "Then the Lord God made a woman from the rib he had taken out of the man and He brought her to the man... man will leave his father and mother and be united to his wife and they will become one flesh." ~ Genesis 2:22-24

who actually cheat) yet an overwhelming majority of Americans believe adultery is morally wrong. Still, they offer a wide array of excuses trying to condone their inappropriate behavior. "I don't love my wife anymore." "I have nothing in common with my spouse." "It was a one-night stand. It meant nothing. It was purely physical."

Infidelity is not limited to a physical relationship - affairs can be emotional or occur even in cyber-space. Former U.S. President, Jimmy Carter, once publically admitted to having *lusted in his heart.* Any thoughts or actions which distract from the intimate commitment between husband and wife are considered a violation of this Commandment. Because one refrains from any actual physical intimacy with an outside party, does that deem the offense any less hurtful or damaging? Ask someone who's spouse had an emotional affair or was caught cheating on the internet. They'll tell you.

"But my spouse doesn't satisfy all my needs so I had to go outside of the marriage." Oh please! Why is it the responsibility of one person to fulfill all of your requirements? Isn't that incredibly demanding and selfish of you? And is it even humanly possible? My husband, as good a person as he is, does not (or can not) give me the emotional support and comfort I seek when I am really hurting. Are there other men in my life I could turn to who would console me in my time of need? I could think of a few but I would never in a million years disrespect my husband by turning to them. (I'm sure my husband considers me lacking as a wife in certain areas as well.) Neither would I offend God and the gift of this union He has blessed us with. Where my husband lacks, God picks up the slack. (That's kind of catchy, isn't it?) God always fulfills my needs when others don't. And if I need a human touch, I can always reach out to one of my girlfriends, sister or Mom, if necessary.

Don't misunderstand - I do not sit in judgment over those who have strayed. Some of the people I love the most have fallen into this trap. This is between them and God, as are all of our behaviors. I am simply stating my feelings pertaining to this Law. As challenging as it may be, individuals must do their best to resist the temptation to covet and work to respect and preserve the sanctity of marriage.

> "So they are no longer two but one. Therefore what God has joined together let man not separate." ~ Matthew 19:6

Let me add, too - those who are single yet seek intimacy with one who is already in a committed relationship must also refrain from this offensive behavior.

Commandment 10

"You Shall Not Covet Your Neighbor's Goods"

Jealousy and envy are two of the most toxic emotions humans feel. Deeply rooted in low self-esteem, poor self-image, insecurity, and feelings of inadequacy, one feels compelled to impress others in an attempt to gain their approval and affirm their own self-worth. Can we truly be content with what we have or do we constantly need to posses what others have?

I first remember designer clothing appearing in stores back in the '80's. There was a frenzy of Jordache, Gloria Vanderbilt, Tommy Hilfiger, and a host of other such garments hanging from the racks in department stores throughout the country. Anyone who was anyone wore designer apparel. Not my kids - they were old enough to know their classmates were spending a fortune to wear ordinary clothing with someone else's name embroidered on their butt. "But all the kids are wearing them, Mom! I'll be totally embarrassed if I show up to school in regular clothes!" "Not going to happen," I explained. "Learn to appreciate and be grateful for what you have. You don't need what everyone else has." This is certainly not an easy lesson for a teenager to learn but a very necessary one indeed.

Years later, when my children began to drive, each purchased their own cars from money they earned and saved during their teenage years. Though having far less monetary value than the parent-purchased Corvettes and Jeeps their peers drove, they were proud of their accomplishments. I'll never forget my oldest daughter stating, "No one *gave* me my car. I earned it myself and I'm proud of that!"

We live in a fast-paced world. It seems as though every few months the current technology we're using becomes obsolete. Every time I turn on the TV or talk to a family member, they're telling me about the latest in cell phones, computers, and assorted gadgets guaranteed to make my life better. I see how easily others replace perfectly good equipment simply because everyone has the latest model and they need to maintain their status among their peers. (I still don't own a dishwasher or microwave. I know I'm strange but I actually like doing dishes.) This competitive need to have what others have overrides our rationale in determining if, in fact, we actually need the item.

But is the final Commandment referring only to material possessions? I don't believe so. It can also refer to being envious of another's friendships, looks, body image, financial position, career, popularity, social standing, and so forth. Jealousy is a poison that contaminates the very fiber of our lives. Like a cancer, it corrupts our sense of well-being, happiness, relationships, and can threaten our life.

Spiritual DWI

I have a family member who is drowning in jealousy towards me. The more successful I become professionally, the more their loathing for me increases. They have bad-mouthed me to family, haven't spoken to me for the better part of my career, and have spread vicious lies to others about me. When confronted with Truth, they refuse to acknowledge it and blatantly proceed in dispersing distorted *facts*. It has destroyed our once tight relationship and infiltrated our entire family unit. Clearly, this individual is not comfortable or secure with themself and feels the need to vilify another in order to raise their status in their own mind and possibly in the eyes of other family members. Ironically, it has done neither.

A combination of Commandments Eight and Ten makes for a lethal cocktail. However, since I do not imbibe, I'm not at risk. Family member "X", however, can be indicted on charges of DWI - Delivering Wrongful Information. It carries a maximum life-sentence of pure misery.

Jealousy could be dramatically reduced if we, as individuals and as a society, removed all competitiveness within our relationships. Jealousy creates a hierarchal existence, placing greater value on some than others. Love removes all distinction and restores balance and equality to all.

While we may believe we are deserving of what others have (I do not measure my worth in material possessions) or that having other than what is currently ours will bring us greater happiness is both adolescent and inaccurate. Envy robs us of the ability to live in gratitude and leads us down the dark road of greed and discontent. Life is not Fox News (fair and balanced) and to desire what others have only leads to heartache, bitterness, and resentment.

Trust -
Aging parent - Jack & Mother
★ interesting concept
Love - want the good for the other person

CHAPTER 6

Walk the Talk

Consider This

In every choice we make, there are several factors we must consider when seeking the answer to "**Does This Please God?**"

First, is the impending decision a serious one? Many are not and don't require much thought. "Should I plant tomatoes or cucumbers?" Don't loose sleep over it.

Second, what are my intentions? Is my decision based on love or malice, kindness or selfishness, fear or compassion for myself and all concerned? This is a critical question not to be taken lightly.

> "Let all that you do be done in love." ~ 1 Corinthians 16:14

Keep in mind that although the bad choices we make are sometimes a path to fulfilling God's Divine Purpose for us, we must take great care in not causing harm to anyone in the process, including ourselves.

> *Think as the mind of God thinks.*
> *See through God's eyes.*
> *Listen with Divine intent.*
> *Align with the Divine.*

Choosing to become a true servant of the Lord is not easy. As with any major life change, enthusiasm reigns high initially. We're all familiar with Born Again Christians deliriously high on God's love, proclaiming His glory to all whom they encounter or a recent college graduate venturing into the corporate world for the first time - blackberry in one hand, IPod in the other - ready to conquer the business sector. Or perhaps the first-time teacher determined to change the world one student at a time. Brimming with hopes and dreams and excitement, they are unstoppable. But as time passes, the realities of the challenges they face begin to emerge. Hope turns to doubt and exhilaration to monotony. It is the passion that first ignited their hearts which enabled them to stay focused and venture onward. But it is commitment to our cause (God) that motivates us forward when we become weary and discouraged.

Square Pegs and Round Holes

I cannot even begin to count the number of people I've known who truly believe they are turning their lives over to God. One such individual is a former client of mine. I met her many years ago in a support group I ran called Reunion of Hearts, Reconciling and Reconnecting Estranged Families. Our group consisted primarily of older parents struggling with the painful separation from their adult children. In each scenario, it was the choice of the child to sever the relationship. Still others had young children snatched away by vindictive exes.

Whatever the case, their pain was beyond definition. All were desperately seeking answers but even more pressing, for reconciliation with their child. Some who were hurting resorted to begging and bribery and others used threats and intimidations. Those of parental alienation turned to attorneys, courts, and political leaders for assistance. Each was trying to force the outcome of their desire.

I worked long and painstakingly hard in accepting and being at peace with (although not happy about) the estrangement from three of my children. While I do not believe God wants us to suffer, I do believe our resistance to that which is meant to be, or to that which we must endure for a higher good, causes our own agonizing pain. Remember, His will is for each of us to come to know and be at one with Him (Peace and Love). The path we take to arrive at that destination (being a good parent or not, living a healthy lifestyle or one of indulgence, receiving a higher education or dropping out of school) is one of our own volition.

> "All things work together for good to them that love God, to them who are the called according to His purpose."
> ~ Romans 8:28

Suffering is the resistance to that which is meant to be or that which we must endure for a higher good.

~

Instead of insisting things work out according to my dictates and trying to squeeze the square peg of reality into the round hole of my selfish needs, I chose to let go and let God. I put my faith and trust in His judgment and handled myself with dignity and love during this entire ordeal. I discovered everything in life is a process. Everything is meant to bring us to exactly where *God* wants us to be next, which is always one step closer to Him, to a deeper place of spiritual awareness, and to ultimately being one with Him in Love. Remember - His will, not mine.

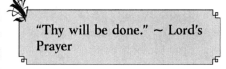

"Thy will be done." ~ Lord's Prayer

I am actually writing this portion of this book from my kitchen table with a pencil and legal pad. (Talk about a blast from the past! That's how I wrote my first six books.) A freak snowstorm on Oct. 29th dumped more than a foot of wet, heavy snow on northwestern N.J. Trees, still adorned with autumn-colored leaves, took down power lines and left hundreds of thousands of homes without power. Day three (of six for me) finds us without electricity - hence, no computer. Thank God for Ticonderoga #2 lead pencils and the lemon-colored pages of Ampads to capture my thoughts and words!

I can type forever in a Word document without breaking stride. My pencil point, however, blunts quickly and needs to be re-sharpened ever twenty or thirty minutes. My sharpener is located at the bottom of the basement stairs. Since I hate writing with a dull point, I repeatedly run up and down the thirteen steps to hone the tip on my writing instrument. So far, that's eight trips in two and a half hours. You would think I love climbing stairs. Certainly, I could have mounted the sharpener in my office like any normal person. But I am far from normal. (You already knew that.) Stairs burn calories, shape and tone calf muscles, and expand lung capacity. *That* I like. So while I'm not overly fond of the *process* I savor the *prize.*

God's process makes my basement stairs look as effortless as riding an escalator. With His Way, many *huff and puff* trying to get in great spiritual *shape*. But keep your eyes on the *prize* because God isn't stingy.

Life According to Burger King

Getting back to my support group - one of the mothers who attended was not in contact with her son for many years. I truly understood her anguish and encouraged her to focus more on her relationship with God and trust Him to work this out according to His way and in His time.

For all the years I've known her, she has resisted God's

"Do not fear, for I am with you. Do not anxiously look about you, for I am your God. I will strengthen you, surely I will help you. Surely I will uphold you with my righteous right hand." ~ Isaiah 41:10

direction time and time again, demanding that only when she is reunited with her child will she be healed. Recently, she returned to church declaring since no one was willing to help her get her child back, she was now turning her life over to God. *Glory hallelujah, praise God*, I thought. My jubilation was quickly squelched when she concluded by saying, *"He'll* get him back for me and then I'll be happy!"

Clearly, she is deceiving herself. The Dalai Lama calls this being a *victim of delusion*. She is not yet ready to commit to God and missed the point completely. Turning your life over to the Master means relinquishing the need to have it your way. That's fine when ordering a cheese burger from Burger King. But in this case it means accepting that God's Way has a higher purpose, even if you are not aware of what it is.

Seek not a quick fix to your suffering.
Realize instead, the higher good and all
misery will subside.

Until and unless she is willing to do this, she will never experience God's peace.

Live By Faith

12/9/20 Stop!

I am thrilled to pieces each time I see my children succeed. To watch them make poor choices and struggle pains me. Yet oftentimes, the struggle is the prelude to their success. My youngest daughter was a single mom for many years. Working multiple jobs, caring for her son, renovating a house and going to school simultaneously left her exhausted, stressed, and financially insolvent. Yet she rarely complained. She kept her eyes on the prize - a better life for her and her son, whatever that might be. Knowing there was a higher purpose to her hardships precluded her from self-pity and defeat. Now, years later, she owns her own business, lives in a beautiful home, is married to a wonderful man (actually, the father of her child) and last year gave birth to her second gorgeous son (with number three on the way!).

She knew God had something wonderful in store for her. Even when things would fall apart, she held tight to that belief. She lived in faith, not fear (most of the time). As parents delight in the successes of their children, so does Father celebrate in ours.

> "Why are you anxious about what to wear? Consider the lilies of the field, how they grow - they toil not, neither do they spin. And yet I say to you, that even Solomon in all his glory is not arrayed like one of these."
> ~ Matthew 6:28-29

Lessons in Fur

Earlier I made reference to the profound love-lessons we learn from our dogs - their innate ability to love and accept us unconditionally. I have been blessed to have had dogs in my life for more than fifty-five years (multiple dogs, not *one* that lived for half a century – just wanted to be clear). My furry companions have taught me much about how God loves. Any dog owner will confirm that our canine buddies love us no matter what - no matter what we look like, no matter our age or level of education, and no matter how sweet or stinky we smell. They love us with pure unadulterated abandon. I mentioned earlier that DoG spelled backwards is GoD referencing their ability to love unconditionally.*

Still, there is another equally as valuable lesson we can and *must* learn from them - dogs live to please their master. Not only are they affectionate and playful but they crave our love and approval and subsequently the rewards for being obedient. All they really care about is making sure we're happy with them.

Yesterday was an unusually long day away from home. I left at 6:15 am to do a TV show in Somerset. From there, I headed north to see clients at the battered women's shelter. I arrived home around 8:30 in the evening. As I pulled in the driveway, I could hear all four of my furry babies barking with delight. "Mommy's home!" (Mommy was equally as happy.) As I approached the back door I could see Butterscotch leaping three feet in the air. Considering she's only about nine inches high at the shoulder and has no Jack Russell in her, that's

---

*   (Check out one of my favorite Youtube videos ever by Wendy Francisco - http://www.youtube.com/watch?v =Hl7edn_RZoY or just log on and search *Dog and God*.)

Unconditional love - Mother
Jack

quite a feat (of which she has four by the way – lame joke, I know. Indulge me). Upon opening the door, the first thing I noticed were pieces of my brand new throw rug scattered all over the floor. "For crying out loud!" I exclaimed. "Who did this? I just bought this rug!" Not knowing for certain who the culprit was (although I have my strong suspicions, Pebbles), I issued a generic reprimand. Wagging immediately ceased, heads hung in shame and a few slithered away in disgrace. "Bad dogs!" I stated firmly. I was not pleased and they knew it.

I'm such a sucker for dogs. I can't look at those adoring brown eyes and stay angry. "Come here", I called. "Mommy loves you anyway!" Without hesitation, they leapt to their feet and scampered over to me, paws sliding every which-way on the porcelain tile floor. Jumping into my arms, they licked my face uncontrollably, tails creating such a breeze as to make me chilly. Pushing at one another to gain my full attention, it was crystal clear all they cared about was pleasing me. Nothing else mattered (ok, maybe kibble but nothing else. Belly rubs, too, but that's it.). It is their greatest joy to be in the good graces of their master. When I am disappointed in their behavior, it causes them great distress, evident in their faces and sullen behaviors.

Every dog I've ever known displays this same trait. Mine continually seek me throughout the day to celebrate our oneness in love and when we are apart, we both feel the emptiness and loss.

Friends have playfully leashed my dogs and tried to lead them away. They instinctively turn to me in fear and hesitation as they brace with resistance. They do not want to be separated from their source of love and sustenance. With me they are safe, nurtured, loved, and well-cared for. There is a bond between us not privy with any other (with the exception of my husband who cares for them equally as tenderly as I do). They continually seek reassurance that our bond is unbroken. Our oneness alleviates fear, magnifies our collective happiness, and intensifies our love.

How, then, do my canine relationships epitomize my relationship with my Creator? I now understand that *my source of joy is my Source of Love* and *my greatest happiness emanates from pleasing my Master*. My life is an extension of Him. He is my Love and Life-force. To disconnect, to fall from His grace, is frightening and creates feelings of distress. I grieve the loss of Oneness and seek to restore it immediately. I have learned, as my dogs have taught me…

> ### The way to enhance my joy and happiness in life is to please my Master.

Dogs please *their* master. I, please *The* Master.

Chocolate Doves

We all relish the approval of others - a boss who congratulates us on landing the biggest contract of the year, our best friend for throwing the surprise party on our milestone birthday or our parents for letting us know how proud they are that we are their children. Being acknowledged by those who are important to us just feels plain good. Feeling good is like Dove chocolate – it's addictive. Once we've tasted it's sweetness we crave more. And the way to feeling good is through right behavior, the kind that pleases God and wins His accolades. This is one addiction I do not need treatment for.

Like our canine companions, making right choices is not always foremost in our mind. Sometimes personal pleasure overrides good judgment. This is why it is

Loving choices for you & others?

accepting God's & loving others.

[handwritten: St Joseph — Trust & Surrender Obedience]

imperative to stay connected to God. My dogs and I are attached by a leash. God's *leash* is that simple four word question, "**Does This Please God?**" Stay connected. Don't let go. You are safe in His care.

If one claims to love the Father, would they not want to please Him again and again? Imagine living life in such a way as to never disappointment the Most High, to continually win His admiration, and to feel the blessings of His favor time and time again? Each time I receive His approval, my level of joy expands immeasurably. "Good job, Janet," is music to my soul. Not only is God pleased but I have actually made a smart choice that serves me well.

> *Every God-based decision yields perfect results. Me and God - perfect together.*

Life's Toughest Question

Very few people, upon arising each morning, actually ask God, "How may I serve you today?" Although I believe most are concerned with living a morally upstanding life, they often navigate each day making rote decisions. Seeking behaviors that feel good in the moment, few may reflect as to whether or not their choices will actually benefit them as well as those around them in the future.

If I was to ask you, and I am, if God is pleased with the manner in which you conduct yourself in the course of a twenty-four hour period, how would you respond? Like those computer surveys with the little circles, on a scale of one to ten, is He *not satisfied, somewhat satisfied or very satisfied*? I have actually queried people with this exact question in some of my workshops. Most instinctively point to their most endearing qualities - "I'm a good father", "I'm always the first at work and the last to leave" or "I get along with everyone (except Jim but no one likes him)". That wasn't my question.

Potholes of Truth

The 1980's and '90's were the most tumultuous time of my life. During that period, I spent a significant amount of time in therapy (not the physical kind – that of mind and spirit). I was blessed to have an amazing spiritual counselor who was knowledgeable, loving, gentle, and tough. She'd call me on my *stuff* if she felt I wasn't facing reality. I recall one specific incident - we were discussing the abusive relationship I was currently in. I spoke of how brutally he hurt me with his hands and words. "I know I don't deserve this," I tearfully stated. "I've never hurt anyone in my life." (Agh! That reeks of self-pity, victimization, and denial - how unattractive!)

"Oh really," Mary inquired rather sarcastically. *Uh-oh*, I thought. *What have I done now?* I hesitated just long enough for her to continue. "And what about the cruelty you imposed on your children when they were young? Are we forgetting about that or doesn't it matter anymore?"

Ouch - that hurt! The reality of the agony and suffering I caused my children stung like a tree branch slapping me across the face in the dead of winter. The ugly truth hurts, like hell. I was painfully aware of what I had done but to openly admit it at that moment triggered years of shame and guilt - emotions I had not yet dealt with or healed. But this proved to be a major turning point in my life. From that moment on, no matter how shameful, frightened or uncomfortable I felt, I was determined to continue my quest of self-truth. More often than not, it has been a treacherous road scattered with hazardous potholes for me to navigate. But the trip has definitely been worth the effort.

> *Authentic self-love can only be attained*
> *through deep personal introspection*
> *and candid revelation of truth.*

Scaling Mt. Everest

Life without challenge is boring. How exciting is it to walk up a hill? Not so much. But to face the task of climbing Mt. Everest is a feat of vast magnitude. (Notice I didn't insert another *feet* joke? You're welcome.) Pushing ourselves to be more, to be better or to accomplish what few dare to attempt brings excitement, confidence, and oftentimes new meaning to our existence. So are you up for the greatest challenge of your life? This will make Mt. Everest look like an ant hill by comparison. Some of you may choose to bail at this chapter. I hope not but if so, perhaps it is not your time. That is between you and your Creator. Remember Mother Theresa's prayer - "It is always between you and God." For those who choose to stay and continue, good luck. You're going to need it. (Just kidding!) You don't need luck so much as courage and resolve. Think of this as you would planning your wedding (but without the big bucks) - lots to think about, tons of stuff to do but the end result is happily-ever-after!

So, for those ready to embark on this leg of your journey, I say "bravo!" It's time to leave your Spiderman Underoos behind, put on your big boy/girl pants and start climbing!

Ice Road Truckers

Have you ever watched the TV show Ice Road Truckers? A camera crew documents extreme truck drivers as they traverse the most bizarre, remote, and dangerous places in the world. Sometimes traveling dirt paths barely wide enough for their big rigs - carved on the side of perilous mountains deficient of guardrails - the only barrier between driver and certain death is a smart judgment call. (This is one challenge I am definitely not brave enough or willing to undertake. I couldn't even watch an entire show I was so nervous!) Now, imagine driving blindfolded. Your only resource is the guide sitting in the seat beside you. He is directing your every move, advising you when to turn right, bear a little to the left, switch gears, slow down or accelerate. *Only* if you believe *unequivocally* that your partner puts your life above his own and is the most highly qualified guide on the planet are you able to close your eyes and relinquish total control to him. It takes an unprecedented leap of faith to put your life into the hands of another. (While All-State claims you're in good hands, I prefer the hands of All-*Mighty*.) As

> "Trust in the Lord with all your heart and lean not unto your own understanding. In all your ways acknowledge Him and He shall direct your paths." ~ Proverbs 3:5-7

> "Cast your cares upon the Lord for He cares about you." ~ I Peter 5:7

time and distance progress, you're confidence in your companion solidifies as each astute resolution reassures you of his competence.

Blind Sided

Accepting the challenge to live the Word can be equally as terrifying to some, dare I say most, because it means relinquishing complete control and living our lives by absolute blind faith.

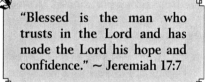

"Blessed is the man who trusts in the Lord and has made the Lord his hope and confidence." ~ Jeremiah 17:7

When I'm comfortable and secure in my job and God directs me to forsake it and follow another path, do I willingly obey or fight Him tooth and nail? If one feels compelled to write a tell-all book about the atrocities they suffered as a child at the hands of their demented parents, would they forgo said desire if instructed by God to quietly forgive them instead?

"In the Lord put your trust." ~ Psalms 11:1

Transcending an egocentric life for a God-centered existence is a foreign concept for many. Most have been conditioned to believe we should live our lives according to our desires, do what feels good, and do what makes us happy. But relinquishing our lives to God does not mean forgoing what we love in exchange for a life of misery. Oh contraire! It means the exact opposite. Focusing on what pleases God actually brings more joy, more satisfaction, more happiness, and more pleasure than we could ever accomplish on our own.

When one embarks on a new venture they are typically advised to start small - baby steps, right? Not so with this. I want you to begin *big*, grab the bull by the horns, reach for the stars, and go for the gusto from the get-go! (That's quite catchy, isn't it? *Go for the gusto from the get-go.* I like that.) I recommend you address the most pressing and serious issues first, working your way down to the lesser ones (if there is such a thing in God's eyes). If you have a drinking problem and also bite your nails, it's a no-brainer – get into AA today and visit your nail tech next month. If you're an absentee parent who's also chronically late to all your appointments, spend time with your children now - address time management at a later date.

The reason being that while every change has value, it is easy to delude ourselves into thinking we are making great progress simply because we forgave the rude cashier in Macy's for having an attitude even though we are approaching the fourth anniversary of not speaking to our mother. Forgiving a relationship of an intimate nature for not repaying a ten thousand dollar loan we made to them takes far more effort than one of a casual nature, say, a ten dollar advance to a neighbor. Rest assured each positive change is pleasing to and acknowledged by God but we must be careful not to credit ourselves for grandiose accomplishments that are, in truth, miniscule by nature.

Who Wants To Be a Millionaire?

As we progress through a series of real life situations, I encourage you to carefully examine each in great detail. Extract it, place it under a microscope and dissect it for any microcosm of validity. Do not rush the process. Spend time, *enough* time, immersed in each scenario, searching and researching for the relativity of each question.

It is the pause between each line that reveals truth, dissipates falsehoods, and restores authenticity.

If you find yourself denying any wrongdoing, imagine Regis Philbin (original host of "Who Wants to Be a Millionaire?") sitting across from you - microphone in hand - asking, "Is that your final answer?" You may need to rethink your response. Just as I stated to Mary that I had never hurt anyone, she gave me a quick dose of reality by asking if I wanted to rethink my reply. In this exercise, like the contestants on WWTBAM, you have three lifelines - a friend, a family member, and one other of your choosing. Those who are closest to us act as mirrors reflecting back to us things about ourselves we may not be aware of – the good and not so good. They can be bluntly honest with us, allowing us to discover truths hidden deep within that we need to be aware of. If you are not certain of the correct answer or if you just want some additional input, reach out to your lifeline and ask how they perceive you. Their response may be far more factual than yours. Make sure to thank them later. (FYI - their response may not necessarily be Truth but rather perception. Both hold great value.)

For those answers that reveal egotism ("yes, I do cheat at poker"), write down a new, love-based response. ("My integrity is now the force that drives my actions.") Vow to make this your default reaction, the one you automatically reach for when presented with that or a similar situation. Do not be misled to believing cheating at a Saturday night card game with your buddies is no big deal. A tiny grain of sand in your shoe is insignificant, too. But we all know, one pebble can cause a painful blister that can become infected, seep into our bloodstream and poison our vital organs. Each *no biggie* has the power to poison our souls and strain our connection to Father.

This is a Test and (Not) Only a Test

Carefully consider each of the following questions. Do you (or have you ever, even once)…

Find fault with everything and everyone?

Have a sense of entitlement ("I shouldn't have to put up with this! I should be able to…")

Been quick to judge an entire nation based on the horrific actions of a few?

Always have to be right, even at the expense of others?

Pressure others to give you what you want, do things your way or be who you want them to be?

Are you controlling and/or demanding?

Live in fear or worry? Are you anxious and nervous?

Struggle with unresolved issues from your past?

Live in the past and have difficulty letting go? ("Ten years ago you humiliated me. I'll never forget that.")

Are you addicted to drugs or alcohol? Do you need them to relax and/or have fun? What about cigarettes, gambling, sex or shopping? Are you addicted to drama?

Are you an absent parent or abusive – verbally, psychologically, physically or sexually? Are you too lenient or permissive, too strict or inflexible?

Are you less than generous (stingy) with your time, money, support, effort or talents? Are you selective with whom you share them? ("I can't stand that old guy up the street so why should I shovel his sidewalk in the winter?")

Only give to those who have something to offer you?

If a stranger was in immediate need of assistance, would you refuse your services claiming it's not your responsibility?

Initiate, spread or engage in rumors? ("Yeah, but everyone does it.")

Are you less than honest (deceitful) with your spouse? (Hide *friendships* on the internet, fail to disclose secret credit card dept or not be truthful with how you really feel about his kids?)

Tell others the *truth* about themselves without regard for their feelings? ("If people can't handle the truth, oh well!")

Outright lie or withhold important information or conveniently *forget* to relay information to the appropriate person? ("I thought you knew we were all meeting at the diner for lunch on Tuesday.")

Seek revenge, get even and have an eye-for-an-eye mentality? After all, that's what the Bible says, right?

Take out your anger on others? ("It's not like I do it on purpose. People just p*ss me off!")

Are you sarcastic or spiteful? (Sarcasm isn't humor, by the way, its passive/aggressive anger.)

Do things for ulterior motives or less than honorable reasons? ("If I kiss-up to my boss, I'll get that promotion.")

Need to gain the approval of others or judge yourself by what others think or say about you?

Don't care what others think of you? (That's actually fear, not self-confidence. If you care and they don't approve it hurts. Remaining emotionally indifferent protects you from the pain of rejection.)

Suffer from low self-esteem and believe you're not *worth it?*

Suffer from over-inflated ego and think you're better than everyone else? (But only because you are, isn't that right?) Deny you have any work to do on yourself? ("There's nothing wrong with me. It's everyone else who needs help.")

Allow others to take advantage of you, use or abuse you or neglect and disrespect you?

Keep peace at all costs?

Believe others must earn your respect, some deserve respect, and some do not? Do you only offer it to those who first extent it to you? (Note from author - the word *respect* means *to value.* Imagine if God only valued those who first respected Him?)

1/23/20

We Interrupt Our Regularly Scheduled Program

How many of the above behaviors do you think please God? Have you answered affirmatively to any? "Yes, I allow others to abuse me, and of course I get even if someone hurts me but it's only to teach them a lesson." (Oh well, gee, in that case God's probably fine with it. I'm being facetious.) Spoiler alert! You need to re-evaluate the way you are living your life. Asking yourself, "**Does This** (my behavior, attitude or beliefs) **Please God?**" will give you vital insights into His Way and allow you to effect positive changes in your behavior. I know - this stuff isn't easy. (I'm sure someone was whining, "But that's hard!") Yes, it's hard but so was learning to walk and do math and build a house but wasn't it all worth it? Look at how you've benefitted from those experiences. Imagine how your life will change from this singular experience?

Back to Our Regularly Scheduled Program

Let's continue. (You thought I was done with you already? Ah, you seriously underestimate me, my friend.) Do you or have you ever…

Watched an injustice occur and done nothing about it? *Wash. D.C., Lincoln Park*

Expected perfection from yourself or others?

Waited for others to make the change before you were willing? ("When he stops being nasty to me I'll be nice to him." Ghandi reminds us "I must first be the change I want to see in others.")

Cover up your mistakes or blame others?

Make excuses for your own bad behavior then judge others for theirs?

Hold grudges?

Use profanity? Do you use God's name in vain?

Are you arrogant, self-righteous, and self-absorbed? Does the world revolve around you?

Are you short tempered, volatile, hostile, and aggressive? "I have a bad temper. I can't help it." (Call me. I can help.)

Are you wimpy, passive, shameful or self-loathing? *Sometimes*
Are you too hard on yourself or don't expect enough?

Are you slow to forgive or refuse completely? Do you believe some don't deserve to be forgiven? (You need to watch www.FromGodWithLove.net - very powerful message!)

Mistreat animals?

Pollute Mother Earth, fail to care for her or over-consume natural resources?

Behave or dress in a provocative way?

Neglect yourself while caring for others? Do you fail to create balance in your life - too much work or too much play?

Are you stressed out, worried or anxious? (Lacking faith in God, are we?)

Are you lazy, unfocused, rude or mean-spirited?

Rely heavily on medications (prescribed or OTC's) rather than seek natural methods of healing?

Derive pleasure from another's suffering? ("But only if it's someone who got what they deserve." That is so not ok!)

Marry for money or prestige or because you *need* someone to take care of you?

Stay in a bad marriage for financial reasons, fear of embarrassment or due to pressure from others?

Brag about your accomplishments?

Have you divorced your spouse because you found someone *better*, drifted apart or *fell out of love*? (Don't even get me started on this one!)

Need to teach others a lesson and/or put them in their place?

Think negatively, are pessimistic or claim literary fame to Murphy's Laws?

Assume the role of innocent victim when bad things come into your life?

Poison the minds of others against someone you have an issue with? Are you guilty of parental alienation?

Sabotage your own chances for happiness or success or ascribe to an *I can't* mentality?

Say hurtful things out of anger or because the other deserved it or believe as long as you apologize afterwards its ok?

That's quite a list. I know I haven't covered all possible examples so feel free to add any of your own I may have missed.

CHAPTER 7

God's All "Right"

Four-by-Four

If you noticed, the above questions fall into four basic categories - the way we treat ourselves, others, our planet, and God. In each, it is vitally important to make certain we are behaving in a way congruent with the heart of God. "**Does This Please God?**" means foregoing ego and residing and behaving exclusively in Spirit. It sometimes means making great sacrifices as well. I want to go on vacation but that means leaving my elderly dad, who lives with me full-time, home alone all week. He is fully capable of caring for himself on a daily basis but grows lonely and fearful when left on his own. Does that mean I must abandon my plans? Perhaps, but not necessarily. Dad's emotional well-being might take precedence over my desire to get away for a fun excursion or it might require hiring someone to stay with him while I'm away. It may also involve shortening my trip to a two-day weekend instead. These types of decisions are deeply personal and unique to those involved. There is no blanket answer other than to choose one performed out of love and concern for all parties, which is the very essence of the heart of God. There is always a way which *Aligns with the Divine* while not causing

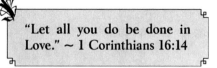

"Let all you do be done in Love." ~ 1 Corinthians 16:14

harm to or ignoring the self or another.

Cheesecakes and Treadmills

A lifestyle change requires a strong commitment despite the endless temptations that infiltrate our daily routines. An impromptu call from friends inviting you to join them for a sumptuous evening at the Cheesecake Factory is declined as you opt for thirty minutes on the treadmill. "A minute on the lips - a lifetime on the hips." You carefully weigh (no pun intended) the consequences of your actions before accepting the invitation, asking yourself "Is this good for me? Will I regret this decision tomorrow when I get on the scale?" Choosing to make *Right-For-Me* decisions is a no brainer once you experienced the rewards assigned to each.

Choosing to make *Right-For-God* lifestyle changes is not always as straightforward for it involves complete faith and surrendering of ego (*Right-For-Me* mindset). Yet once you've experienced the freedom and exhilaration of forgiving someone who betrayed you, it's hard to imagine carrying the burden of a grudge ever again. When you view difficult people as children of the Most High struggling with unresolved issues and relinquish all judgment of them, you never again label them jerks, idiots, worthless, and such. When you resist telling your ex what a sorry excuse he is for a man and bad-mouthing him to his children, family, and friends, you will savor the joy of maintaining your personal integrity and allowing the natural relationship between him and those important to him to remain intact.

In the thirty years since my divorce, I have never spoken unkindly about my ex. I made the decision the day he left to continue to love him. After all, I did so for eighteen years and those qualities I admired are still present in him. I've never damaged his reputation or relationships regardless of what transpired between us. I am pleased (as I know God is) to say I kept my word. I am candid about sharing some of the things he's done without debasing him as a person. His behavior is independent of who he is intrinsically. I take great care in keeping them separate. I may comment on his behavior while acknowledging him for the good person he is. *Right-For-God* choices exempt us from regret, remorse, shame, guilt, and the effects of bad decisions.

> ### *"A moment of immorality results in a lifetime of consequences."*

RFG lifetime benefits consistently outweigh *RFM* momentary satisfactions. Understand though, this can only be attained when one maintains complete and enduring faith in the Lord. Too often, we know the *RFG* answer yet rationalize our way out of or around it.

Muddy Floors and Kids

"I know kids will be kids and stuff will get ruined but for cryin'out loud - every time I turn around someone's tracking mud in on their shoes! So, I blew up and started screaming at them. They know I don't mean it. I know it wasn't right but I'm only human. Everyone yells at their kids. At least I don't beat them like some parents. They'll get over it. And besides, when they clean up the mess and I've calmed down I'll apologize."

God certainly understands. After all, He's a parent and just look at the huge mess His kids have made on His property. Certainly, if anyone has just cause to throw a hissy fit, He does. Yet instead, He gently helps us recognize the error of our ways. I have yet to hear Him curse, threaten or berate anyone.

As for the kids - who says they'll understand? Isn't that statement meant to relieve me of guilt and from having to look at myself and make personal changes? Do not deceive yourself for one instant that because you love them and say you're sorry it erases the wounds inflicted on them. It doesn't. I know - I hurt my children and their pain lingered for years and may exist even today. An apology can initiate the healing process but doesn't it make far more sense to simply avoid inflicting pain at all?

You can drive a nail into a piece of wood, remove it, and patch the hole. But the wood remains forever damaged.

While God applauds a sincere act of contrition, don't be too quick to pat yourself on the back just yet. Take a moment before lashing out and rethink your options. Ask yourself, "What behavior would be most pleasing to God?" and follow through. Then give yourself a big well-deserved hug.

In The Secret side of Anger, I provide a three-step process for those who have explosive anger issues. It's called the SWaT Strategy. When you feel angry, Stop what you're doing, Walk away to compose yourself, and Talk yourself calm. When shifting from an *RFM* mentality to an *RFG* mindset, you can make a simple adjustment to SWaT - Stop what you're doing, Walk away to buy some time, and Talk to God. Ask Him what will please Him the most? SWaT - Stop, Walk and Talk - easy to remember, protects all parties from harm, and allows for a love-based response.

Back to the muddy floors - you can still address the issue at hand but now do so from a perspective of being assertive and reasonable. Polite and firm trumps abusive and apologetic every time.

Let me state, there is a difference between knowing *RFG* answers and actually putting them into practice. Most of us know right from wrong. Not as many apply it.

Sensitivity Disorder

In my twenties, I was stricken with a condition called *Sensitivity Disorder*. Symptoms included getting my feelings hurt easily, oversensitivity to the criticisms and negative comments from others, taking things personally, an inability to release pain, and dangerously low self-esteem. Ok, there really is no such disorder. I just made it up. My first husband called me *moody* and to him that's probably what it seemed like. No one likes a moody person. But in my younger years I was unaware as to how to protect myself from another's hurtful comments, especially his. I believed others *made* me feel a certain way. Now I know I choose my own feelings.

As is true with all of us, sometimes he would say or do things that were insensitive or unkind. I don't believe he deliberately meant to hurt me and was unaware of how his actions were affecting me. Regardless of his intent, my feelings were easily crushed. Long after the behavior had ended, I was unable to move beyond my pain. I held on to it for days or weeks at a time. Even though he had long since forgotten what transpired and had resumed his normal niceties, I was unable to appreciate and acknowledge him. I know there were times I failed to recognize him for his thoughtfulness and I'm sure that hurt him as well. And I also know I disappointed God on at least two levels. First, I was stuck in my own misery - God did not create me to suffer. Second, my husband deserved to be credited for the good person he is. All acts of kindness deserve to be rewarded, at the very least, with a verbal expression of gratitude.

Captain Brainiac and the Case of the Vanishing Anniversary

Fast forward twenty-some years - I have completely overcome Sensitivity Disorder as I have outgrown ego. I am happy to say I now predominantly reside in Spirit and am more concerned with how God wants me to treat others than with how I am currently feeling at that precise moment. Spirit is alive and well in my current marriage to my second husband.

Mac has never been one who assigned much importance to birthdays, holidays, anniversaries, and such. He is, you could say, less-than-sentimental. For the most part, I have removed all expectations and unspoken demands of him. I choose, instead, to focus my energies on loving and appreciating him exactly the way he is. After all, isn't this the only way to love – freely and without limits and demands - as God loves us?

Therefore, I am rarely disappointed or angry with him. I say rarely because, admittedly, I sometimes allow ego to override Spirit. (Reduced expectations result in reduced anger.) Let me share with you a time I screwed up because Lord knows I do not want you to think I have ascended to a state of perfection quite yet. I still have a long way to go.

Our fourteenth wedding anniversary came and went with virtually no recognition from him. Much to my dismay, I found myself mildly irritated by his indifference. I remained relatively quiet as enemy forces disguised in fatigues of self-pity strategically planned a sniper attack on my heart. However, my Commander in Chief was on high alert and immediately deployed troops to ward off an offensive (and believe me, self-pity is highly offensive). How dare I feel sorry for myself because I married a man who works hard, doesn't abuse me, hasn't had an affair, makes me laugh hysterically, built a house for my daughter with no personal gain, is loved, admired and respected by all who know him but doesn't assign much hoopla to man-made festivities. Oh, the inhumanity!

I managed to avoid a direct hit but the enemy was still lurking and I needed to regroup. I reached for my *weapon of mass con-struction* - love. Rather effortlessly, I worked my way out of arrogance and self-righteousness and back to Spirit. Later that evening when Mac invested two and a half hours of his time dismantling my rug shampooer to find out why it wasn't siphoning water out of my carpet, I was able to express my deep gratitude for undertaking yet another dirty job. Rather than just a flippant "thanks", I proceeded to elaborate on how invaluable my Hoover is to me. With four long-haired dogs it's an absolute God-send. Once again, *Captain Brainiac* to the rescue! (That's the moniker his co-workers assigned him as he has a God-given ability to resolve even the most challenging mechanical issues.) I issued a resounding "Ta-ta-da-da" (the triumphant sound super heroes make when they save the day). This playfulness makes him laugh and, more importantly, shows him how much his efforts mean to me.

I really like myself when I am able to put aside my own self-centeredness and respond in love to another, especially in a difficult situation. Like anything else, this response becomes easier the more we practice it and eventually - hopefully - becomes habitual.

Redefining Love

Regardless of whom we are dealing with, what they have done or failed to do, said or omitted, regardless of their agenda or attitude or whether or not we even like them, God requires we love all His children as He loves. No excuses - no if's, and's, but's or when's. Keep in mind, to love does not require I approve of the way a person behaves or the manner in which they live their lives. Behavior is not who they are. To love is to see God within. It is not a feeling or word but the way in which we treat one another. I wrote the following in 1996 for my wedding...

My Thoughts on Love

Some people think love is a feeling, an emotion, something that you fall into, and sometimes fall out of, something that just happens, something you can't control.

I believe love is so much more than that. I believe love is very definitely a feeling, but not exclusively a feeling. Love is also a decision, a behavior, a conscious choice.

What first stirs feelings of love within us for another is recognizing the beauty, the goodness, the specialness that God created within that person. The beauty never changes, the specialness never diminishes. Sometimes we just lose sight of it. Sometimes we focus on a person's behavior - they may be acting angry, depressed, selfish, defensive or sarcastic. It is the behavior that we dislike. But the behavior is not the person. They are two very separate entities and we need to remember to keep them separate.

The reason why we sometimes feel we have "fallen out of love" is because we choose to focus on the person's behavior rather than on who they are intrinsically. We loose sight of the very essence of who they are and that essence is God. And God is pure love.

To love someone is to recognize and honor God's presence within.

Loving someone means not only feeling love but also treating that person in a loving way every day. To love someone is to care enough about them to do what is best for them, even when the feeing of love is not apparent. This takes a conscious effort. This is the decision to love.

To say "I love you" is easy. To live "I love you" is not. Relationships are not about being in love. Relationships are about becoming a loving person. And to become a loving person is the greatest reward in life.

To become a loving person is the greatest reward in life.

To become God-like (Love) is life's greatest accomplishment.

Linkedin to Love

Recently I posed the following question to a group of my colleagues in one of my Linkedin groups, "What is greater - to be loved or to love?" The vast majority responded "to be loved". It has been my experience that most people seek to *be* loved. They search for someone who finds them attractive, makes them happy, and tells them they are special. Certainly it is reassuring to know someone finds me desirable. However, it takes no effort on my part for someone to love me. This is purely an expression of their personal preference. I could be the nastiest, laziest, most self-centered woman on the planet and if someone wants to love me they will. (We all know a couple where one party is obnoxious and we wonder *what does she/he see in him/her?*) Conversely, no matter how sweet, kind, or thoughtful I am, that same individual could despise me. The truth about who I am has nothing much to do with it. People choose to see something unique within another that attracts them or not.

But for me to love others, well, that's a horse of a different color (no lame joke about colorful horses - you're welcome). Some people are easy to love, others take more effort. It takes relatively little energy to feel affection for someone who treats me well, is kind, polite, and thoughtful. However, to care about someone who is jealous of me, ignores me, is rude and disrespectful or outright hurtful, now that requires some serious God-pleasin' energy!

But look at the rewards - first, I resist the temptation to be adversely influenced by another's troubled behavior which naturally makes me a stronger person. Second, I develop my ability to be more compassionate and less judgmental (God-like qualities), both of which expend far less energy than their counterparts. Third, I remove all expectations placed on that individual to live up to who I think they should be, allowing me to live in peaceful coexistence with them (fewer expectations equal less anger, remember?). Fourth, I deepen my capacity to love and who benefits from that? I do! We all love rewards. We expect them from our credit card company, we cash in our frequent flyer miles, and we open bank accounts for that free tote bag. In each case, we have to spend money to redeem them. In this instance we don't have to spend a dime. Priceless!

I love nature, I love music, and I really love chocolate. I cannot recall a single instant when I felt that love being reciprocated. The simple act of loving brings me immense joy and for that reason alone, I want to love more. If it is mutual, that's great but it is not mandatory. My feelings are not contingent upon theirs.

*Seek not to be loved. Rather, live to love
like God.*

Dominoes Delivers

In addition to experiencing greater ease and serenity in your life, an added perk of being a more loving person is the domino effect it has on others. When you are brimming with God's love, kindness, generosity of spirit, forgiveness, hope, joy, and compassion this is precisely what you offer each person you encounter throughout your lifetime. Imagine how wonderful it would be and how life-affirming to present these gifts to every contact you make. Imagine, too, the global impact it could have on the world's entire population. Attitudes are contagious so be a carrier! Whether family or stranger, friend or enemy, lover or ex- all are children of the same Heavenly Father, my brothers and sisters, all equal in value to Him. Do not discriminate or show favoritism. Infect everyone with Love!

I am currently reading a book about the life of the Dalai Lama. When China infiltrated his beloved Tibet and committed horrific atrocities against his people, he chose to respond with *Ahimsa* – non violence. It is one of the very tenets of Buddhism. His Holiness states that his religion is kindness. Imagine if the entire world was baptized in kindness?

"But, the whole world isn't kind, Janet!" someone states angrily. "So why should I be?" Well, the entire world isn't healthy, either, or financially stable or adventurous or smart. But does that deter you from becoming what benefits you most simply because others aren't? Again, your life is between you and God. Be an inspiration to the world.

Karma's Kickin' Butt

About four years ago a woman named "Maureen" arrived at our shelter. Having recently escaped an abusive marriage she was justifiably angry, stressed, fearful, and very bitter. She wore her emotions on her sleeve and made no excuses for her arrogance and hostility. As with all shelter residents, attending my anger management group is mandatory. She was not happy and made no bones about it.

Sitting as close to the exit door as possible without being in violation of the township fire code, she refused to participate. Arms folded tightly across her chest, body facing the door, her attitude clearly disturbed the other women who, while also unhappy about being there, were at least behaving more appropriately. "She's disrespecting you, Miss Janet!" they complained. "I'm ok", I reassured them. "I don't take it personally. She doesn't want to be here but at least she showed up." As was customary, I always began and ended each meeting by expressing my appreciation to those who attended.

The meetings are informal and everyone is encouraged, though never pressured, to share. Criticisms and judgments of one another are not permitted. Each is instructed to speak of their own experiences. I frequently interject facts about anger along with techniques to better manage it more effectively and ultimately heal it. I emphasize the importance of choosing to live a more peaceful life. My words are always consistent with my spiritual beliefs and I freely speak about my relationship with and love of God. For the most part, the ladies are pretty receptive.

"I don't believe in all that God crap", Maureen sneered one evening. "There is no such thing as God. If there was, He wouldn't let me get beat up." She seemed poised for a fight. The others gasped in disbelief. A few immediately jumped to my defense (not that I required it).

"Wait a minute," I instructed them. "Everyone here is entitled to their own beliefs and we all need to respect that." A potential riot had been temporarily averted. "Have you always been an atheist?" I inquired. "What is it like not to believe in a Higher Power?"

Maureen shared a glimpse of her past. Raised a Christian, she lost faith in God upon finding herself married to a man who brutally beat and tortured her every day. Threatening to kill their children if she refused him, her logic led her to dismiss the notion of a benevolent Being who supposedly loved and protected us. Her bruised body was proof enough no such Being existed. She was angry and hurt. My heart went out to her.

"I am so very sorry you had to endure that, Maureen, but I'm happy you're here with your children and safe at last. I'll do whatever I can to help you get back on your feet." She shot me a cynical look of distrust. Baby steps…

I am not in the business of trying to convert people - not to my way of thinking, my beliefs or my faith. I simply share. I liken myself a gardener planting seeds. Whatever germinates will grow. What lies dormant, well, perhaps now is not the right time. Whoever likes what they hear is free to take it and apply it. If not, I let it be. Perhaps I am not the source they can relate to or perhaps my information is not what they currently (or ever will) need. Either way, I'm ok with their decision.

Each week, Maureen faithfully showed up for our group. I was grateful she did and let her know. Each week, I shared my faith while respecting where she was in her journey. And each week, she became a little more comfortable with me, letting her guard down ever-so-cautiously. As time passed, I noticed her chair moving further away from the exit and a bit closer to me until one evening she was sitting directly in front of me. The tension in her body eased, her face was noticeably more relaxed, and her voice more enthusiastic. She seemed more receptive to my words and inquired about my relationship with God.

There was a hint of melancholy in her voice. "I wish I had what you have, Janet", she said. "Open your heart to Him, Maureen. He so wants to be a part of your life. He wants to bless you and heal you of your suffering and make you whole. Don't fight Him." Her eyes never left mine. She wrapped her arms tightly around me and whispered, "Thank you so much." "My pleasure, Maureen, my pleasure." Ah, what a little kindness and patience will do! God was pleased.

The Sequel

Nice story but it doesn't end there. A few weeks later, she came into my office, bubbling with excitement. "I'm leaving, Janet! I got an apartment and a job! I cannot thank you enough for all you've done for me." Appreciation - it glows like warm embers in the heart. "I'm thrilled for you", I stated. I truly was though I must selfishly admit I was sad to see her go. I had become quite fond of her and would miss her. "Where will you be working?" I inquired. "Well, I'm a registered nurse and I got a job at Oakland Care Center." My mouth dropped to the floor. "No way! My dad has Alzheimer's and we just moved him into that nursing home." (What are the odds?) "What's his name", she asked. "I'll make sure he gets special treatment." Talk about karma!

It's not easy dealing with difficult, arrogant, and angry people. I do it for a living so I have to be professional. Regardless of whether I'm in business or personal mode, it is always foremost in my mind to treat God's precious children in a manner consistent with His Way. By operating from a place of Spirit, I know unequivocally I have made a *Right-For-God* choice and feel good about myself. God is pleased, the other party benefits, and I am happy with who I am. All rewards - no consequences. What a way to live!

CHAPTER 8

The Spiritual Millionaire

Microscopic Living

Now that you've been brutally honest with yourself (kudos, by the way – I know how hard that was), let's begin the process of becoming a spiritual millionaire. Let's randomly review some of your answers to the previous questions for elements of truth. Too often, truth is buried under fear - "I don't want to admit I have a drinking problem. It's embarrassing." But fear impedes our ability to live fully in the Lord and condemns us to a life of disappointment and mediocrity. Dissecting each answer for any minutiae of truth is the first step towards freedom and a God-based life.

Your acknowledgement of each truth is subsequently followed by a big hug (from God to you) along with a sample affirmation - a written and spoken commitment to making a favorable change signifying your spiritual rebirth. Please feel free to write your own if those I have provided do not resonate.

Keep in mind - in each of these challenges, our goal is always to behave and live in a manner pleasing to the

Father. Is He satisfied with our current attitudes and actions and if not, what changes would *He* like to see?

One For the Money... *Controlling with love*

"Are you controlling and/or demanding?" If you answered no, permit me to challenge your answer. (Actually, I don't need your permission. I'm just being polite.) For the most part we are all pretty much control freaks. We want things to be a certain way and as long as they move in our direction, we're content. But if something or someone is not what or who I want them to be, I get angry and upset. I may put pressure on them, coerce, lay guilt upon, bribe, argue with or threaten in order to get my way.

"But," you say, "it's only because my way is the right way." To that I respectfully reply, '"Oh really, and who even cares?" More often than not, being right is a matter of ego. When dining in a fine restaurant, do you eat your salad with the designated fork? I don't. I use one fork for everything. My friend became upset with me one evening. "You can't do that!" she stated. "You're supposed to use the salad fork. That's what it's there for." My reply that I was perfectly content using the larger fork didn't ease her embarrassment. She tried pressuring me to comply with her rules of etiquette but I simply ignored them. Believing she was only following proper protocol, she failed to see herself as controlling. I, on the other hand, did as soon as she was unwilling to accept my decision.

We're all familiar with the *my-way-or-the-highway* guy - rigid, unyielding, demanding, and arrogant, or the nagging wife and bickering spouses who nitpick the most insignificant issues. These are perfect examples. Like a tree that bends with the wind, God wants us to be more flexible and accepting.

Greek } *languages*
Aramaic } *of Christ*

Affirmation: *"All is as it is meant to be and I am comfortable in the knowledge I am a child of the Most High."*

The Texas Two-Step D.C. Park

"Watch an injustice occur and do nothing about it?" How many times are we aware of an unfairness or injustice taking place and sit idly by doing nothing to correct it? It's obvious your niece is favored over her younger brother yet you don't address it with your sister for fear of creating a rift. A co-worker is wrongly accused of a mistake that cost the company their largest account. You know of their innocence yet don't want to get involved. After all, it's none of your business.

Do we think God is pleased when we refuse to take a stand for what is fair and just? If I was the one being mistreated, wouldn't I appreciate someone coming to my aid? While it is not always convenient, I am my brother's keeper in the sense that we all have a moral responsibility to ensure the well-being and care of one another.

Affirmation: *"I am my brother's keeper and my love propels me into action."*

Triple Play

"Live in fear and worry? Are you anxious and nervous?" At one time or another we've all been worried about something - the health of our unborn child, finances, whether or not we'll be accepted by the college of our choice, loosing a loved one or changing careers. Some worry to the extreme - resulting in migraines, ulcers, skin conditions or high blood pressure, loosing

Fear is natural

sleep, a decline in the ability to enjoy life, and much more.

When my youngest daughter bought her first house, she was understandably nervous. She fluctuated between excitement over the thought of having a home for her son to grow up in to worrying about how she was going to afford the monthly expenses and maintain it on her own. It saddened me because I was fully confident she would be fine. (I know my daughter.) I continually reassured her that not only did I believe in her capabilities but if ever she needed anything, my husband and I were there to help. She trusted my words and signed the papers in her attorney's office. I would never have supported her in doing something I knew would be detrimental to her. I believed buying this house was a smart investment. All I cared about was her happiness and well-being. So it is with God - He wants us to trust Him and an absence of trust leads to fear and worry. Will things always work out the way I planned? Of course not. Trusting in God means He

> "I will instruct you and teach you in the way you should go, I will counsel you and watch over you." - Psalm 32:8

always has my back. He will either remove the hardship from my path or give me everything I need to face it head-on. Trusting God allows me to live anxiety-free - in other words, peacefully. Try it. You'll see. Let go of worry. Live in faith.

~

Affirmation: "God resides in my heart. There is no room for fear. I am at peace."

Four Score…

"Have a sense of entitlement ("I shouldn't have to put up with this. I should be able to…")." This attitude seems to be a generational affliction which has infected society in general. I first noticed it in my children during their teenage years and quickly put a halt to it. Where this arrogance originated I'm not certain nor is it important to me. Why would anyone think they are exempt from what the rest of the world has to endure? "I shouldn't have to clean up someone else's mess." And yet haven't we all found ourselves in that very situation at some point in our lives? To the best of my knowledge, there is no eleventh commandment that states, "Thou shalt not have to put up with unfairness in thy life."

I have a friend who continually refers to me as *lucky*. (Because as everyone knows - I haven't worked hard at all for the success I've achieved.) "You're lucky you're thin, have a wonderful career, and have a husband who's a really nice guy." "It's not luck" I explain. "God just loves me more than you." (Just for the record - I never actually said that… out loud. That's so ridiculous sounding I almost couldn't even type it.) Nothing in my life has ever been handed to me. I've had to work hard for everything I have and I've dealt with plenty of sh*t along the way. But you know what they say about manure - it makes excellent fertilizer! I used my *manures* to grow.*

No one is exempt from dealing with injustice, unfairness, inconveniences, and such. I'm of retirement age yet many in my generation aren't afforded the luxury of leaving their jobs due to depleting Social Security

---

*   (Read "Why Me and Tomatoes" on my website @ http://
     www.pfeifferpowerseminars.com/ppsl-newsletter.
     html#tomatoes.)

funds coupled with a bad economy. This is one of our injustices to endure. Sad, but every generation has challenges unique to them.

Arrogance contradicts humility. Jesus washed the feet of His twelve Apostles so who am I to complain when asked to be obedient?

Affirmation: *"The world does not revolve around me. I cheerfully accept unexpected hardships into my life, never losing focus of the many ways God continually blesses me."*

High Five

"Been quick to judge an entire nation/ethnic group based on the actions of a few?" If you're old enough to read this book you've lived through 9/11. Prior to that date, I was unaware of anyone in the U.S. having an issue with people of Middle Eastern descent. Yet immediately following the horrific events of that day, some Muslims residing in this country were terrified to leave their homes. There were reports of innocent Pakistanians being targeted with violence. African Americans, Mexicans, and other ethnic groups know what it feels like to be judged and mistreated based on the shocking actions of the minority.

We classify people based on political affiliations ("all democrats/republicans are..."), gender, age, and religious beliefs (or not) rather than address each on an individual basis. Do you judge all women as gold-diggers because your ex-wife misappropriated all of your assets or teenagers as promiscuous, lazy drug users based on what you read in the newspaper? Sadly, how we judge a person is reflected in the way we treat them, regardless of who they are. Rather than see others collectively as a unit, we need to know and value each autonomously.

God knows what is in the heart of each of His beloved and doesn't judge. We are reminded to follow His example.

Affirmation: *"I remove all labels and pre-conceived notions of my brothers. Each is a unique creation of the Almighty."*

Six Pack

"Find fault with everything and everyone?" One of my clients is the nicest guy you'd ever want to meet but he is miserable and unhappy. He cannot see the good in anything and continuously finds things to criticize. Whether it's the weather, his job, the new car he purchased or a project his working on, he lacks the awareness of how to live in gratitude and consequently has a warehouse full of suffering and grief. I kid him (although I'm serious) that when he finally wins the multi-million dollar lottery, he'll complain because the government took 60% of it. So sad - he fails to see all God has and continues to bless him with each day.

Are you consumed with bitterness towards your much younger supervisor who everyone knows only got the promotion over you because of her cleavage? When the landscapers left, rather than compliment them for how nice your lawn looks, did you point out how they failed to trim around the tree in the far left back corner of your property? But perhaps your complaints are not exclusive towards others. Are you overly critical of yourself? When you gaze into a mirror, do your eyes immediately fixate on the body parts you are least happy with?

Affirmation: *"Perfection belongs to God. I see God in everyone and everything. I am content and grateful for what is."*

Stop !

Lucky Seven

"Always have to be right, even at the expense of others?"
I enjoy reading advice columns in the daily newspaper. I've been a fan of Dear Abby since I was in my teens. However, I get weary reading about someone who had a disagreement with a spouse, friend or co-worker and wants Abby to tell them who's right. The topic that generated the most mail ever was "What is the correct way to hang a roll of toilet paper?" (I'm not making this up – honest!) "Should it be draped over the top or pulled from beneath?" Are you kidding me? This is what people argue over? It was a heated debate that lasted several months.

In my conflict resolution workshop, I address communication skills. I strongly advise people to eliminate the words *right* and *wrong* from their vocabulary. Needing to prove someone wrong is ego-based. I'll venture to say that 99.999% of all issues have not one iota to do with *rightness*. They are matters of opinion, perception, feelings or needs. Save for issues of morality or absolute fact ("No, I am not Jewish, I'm a Christian"), omit both words. Unless of course, you want to admit your mistake and give credit to the other. "Opps, my mistake. You were correct when you said the Giants won the Super Bowl in 2012."

My friend searched for and married "Mr. Right". You may know him - his first name is "I'm Always". She's never won an argument yet but she keeps trying. You've just got to love her determination!

Do you make a point of proving your correctness even at the risk of embarrassing or humiliating the other party? At your uncle's surprise 100th birthday party, you made a point of letting everyone know you found proof he was actually born in 1913, not 1912 as he claimed. "He's ninety-nine, not 100!" you proudly exclaim. "I told you so!" Of course everyone present, especially the guest of honor, is eternally grateful for your candidness. They quickly retrieve their gifts as they head for their cars, leaving behind a mortified old man and the children who planned his special event.

Inflicting disgrace and shame on another is cruel and inhumane. It violates one of God's most sacred teachings - love others as you love yourself.

Annoying Neighbors

Recently my husband and I went out to dinner with another couple. Married longer than we have been, these two engaged in a *right-fighting* competition, determined to prove who was more correct. The subject of annoying neighbors came up. "The guy who lives next door to us is a jerk," she stated. "No he's not", the husband replied. "He's a nice guy." "No he isn't" she insisted. "He cut down all the trees dividing our properties. Now we have no privacy." "Yeah, but that doesn't mean he's not nice," the husband countered. "Yes it does," she argued. "He should have checked with us first!" It continued for several more minutes until the waiter interrupted us for our order. Instead of allowing each their own opinion, they engaged in a battle of ego as each became increasingly more annoyed with the other. *RBG* thinking allows for each to maintain their individual perspective without feeling threatened by the other.

> Affirmation: *"Before I speak, I examine my words and motives making sure they always reflect God's love."*

Eight is Enough Already

"Live in the past? Have difficulty letting go?" ("Ten years ago you cheated on me. I'll never forget that.") By

far, the topic I lecture on which resonates the most with me is the Healing Power of Forgiveness. The majority of people who attend are those who have difficulty forgiving someone who wronged them. It is not uncommon to meet someone who has held a grudge for years, sometimes decades. We may feel the need to be vindicated and impose suffering on the one who hurt us. (What goes around comes around so technically I'm just helping the process along.) We erroneously believe that if we are hurting, the way to heal our pain is to inflict it on another. And yet that makes about as much sense as saying if I have a cold I can get rid of it by giving it to someone else. We all know that is obsurd. We simply have two people who are now both sick.

So it is with resentment. Who benefits? No one. The hater may feel powerful but in reality they are being held captive by the past. The other may feel shame or sadness or not be affected at all. In either case, God sees a damaged relationship where one could have flourished or at the very least, found peace with the other. Each could have chosen to benefit from the experience but instead have built a wall of bitterness between them. On a global level, this poison infiltrates society, festers, and manifests in multiple areas. A world created in love falls prey to acrimony. This is not pleasing in God's eyes at all. Put down your burdens. Heal your heart. Bring healing to others.

We cannot be a world at peace until we are first a people of peace.

~

Affirmation: "I have learned from the past and release it. I now live in the present as I prepare for eternity."

Nine Lords-A-Leaping

"Need to gain the approval of others? Judge yourself by what others think or say about you?" As I mentioned previously, I used to suffer from dangerously low self-esteem. As a result I became a master people-pleaser. I spent the major (certainly not the better) part of my life measuring my worth against what others thought of me. As long as they approved, I felt some glimmer of value. In my forties, I took a course on self-esteem and I must say it did help. But one day it occurred to me that God wants me to see the beauty He created in me and honor it. I thought back to the '70's and a poster I had seen at a retreat - "God don't make junk," it stated. I always remembered it but was unable to apply it to myself. When I related it to how I would feel if my beautiful children didn't love themselves, it changed my perspective.

When you are unable to feel good about who you are, you live in a state of depression, unhappiness, and despair - unable to fully enjoy your life. How you feel about yourself impacts every aspect of your life. People with low self-esteem are statistically less happy and successful than those who enjoy a healthy sense of self.

I also realized that failure to love myself was an insult to the One who created me. In essence, I was criticizing God's handiwork. God is incapable of mistakes, imperfections or *irregulars*, so-to-speak. Everything and everyone created by His hand is flawless and for me to dispute that point is offensive and rude.

My Creator reveals the Truth about me - I am intrinsically perfect. (My behavior, which is learned, may leave a lot to be desired. However, I can unlearn the bad and replace it with that which is pleasing to Father.) While others may feel qualified to express their so-called truth to me, in essence it is opinion and perception. And while I can learn a lot about myself based on what others see, it is does not define who I am and what I am worth. Acceptance and approval from others is flattering but the only position that ultimately matters is God's.

Affirmation: *"I am created in the image and likeness of God. His love for me is sufficient."*

A Perfect Ten

"Pressure others to give you what you want, do things your way or be who you want them to be?" With the help of my therapist many years ago, I was able to see my own coercive tendencies. I realized bribing, pressuring, threatening or inflicting guilt or shame on others were all forms of manipulation. While I had never considered myself manipulative (after all, I'm such a nice person), she readily pointed out one area where I tried to shame a friend. "I can't understand why you always break your promises to me? I've never done that to you." (Ooh, reeks of guilt!) I was trying to shame her into seeing the error of her ways while making myself look saintly. Unaware of my intentions (as we so often are), I wanted her to feel bad so she would change her behavior. I'm certain God was not pleased that I chose such a hurtful way to express how I wanted her to treat me. A simple "It's important to me that you keep your word" is a more direct and respectful approach.

Did I tell you the story of trying to convert my husband to a romantic? No? You'll like this – it's a perfect example of how we pressure without realizing. When we first married, I thought I could teach him to be romantic. How ridiculous does that sound? He had built the most beautiful fireplace in our living room so one evening I set the stage and invited him to join me in front of the open fire. Candles lit, soft music, big squishy throw pillows on the floor - "Come sit", I said. "Why?" he questioned. "So we can talk." "About what?" "Us," I whispered in a sultry voice. His eyes glazed over as his chin fell into his chest. (Have you ever seen the videos on Youtube about the fainting goats? Oh, you've got to see them - they're hysterical! When these goats get scared, their bodies stiffen up and they fall over as though they're dead. My husband reminded me of a fainting goat.)

I don't know what ever possessed me to try to coerce this man into becoming something he clearly never was and has no desire to be. Looking back, I wonder what God must have thought about my ploy. Did He think it was a good idea? "Way to go, girl! I clearly made a defective man so by all means make some improvements." I released him from my ruse and sent him back to the comfort of the bedroom TV. It took me a bit longer before I realized my role in this marriage was to appreciate, accept, and enjoy him exactly as he is. God doesn't need my help fixing his *defective* children, especially since I haven't fixed all of my own defects yet.

"My children will all go to college. I won't have it any other way." "If we can't go to the Bahamas for vacation, then you can just go without me!" (Go - you may enjoy yourself more.) "This is *my* house and you'll do as I say!"

The world and those who inhabit it are not here to live up to my expectations and cater to my demands. Let people be who they are. If that does not work for you, simply state how you feel (if you must) and how you would prefer things to be. If they, or the situation, change, fine. If things remain status quo, can you be ok with it for now? If not, perhaps it's time for you to let go and move on without resentment.

Affirmation: *"I release the need to have things my way. I accept and appreciate what is, knowing I am always fine."*

Oceans Eleven

"Tell others the "truth" about themselves without regard for their feelings?" (If people can't handle the truth, too bad!) Most people I know truly believe they are only being honest with the other party because they care and because the other person simply must know the truth. More often than not, our truth is our opinion or perception. "You only care about yourself and you use people," may be my observation but am I seeing the complete picture? I may not be privy to the individual's kindnesses and generosities when they are extended. And their motives for befriending someone are pure conjecture on my part. No one can accurately say *why* someone is behaving in a particular manner.

There are times when being fully honest with someone is necessary. ("You have a drinking problem.") However, there are two types of honesty - brutal and polite. Brutal honesty has no concern what-so-ever for the feelings of the other party. It blurts things out in a blunt, coarse, and often hurtful manner, and can be highly offensive. Polite honesty, by contrast, speaks Truth while carefully considering how the other may feel upon hearing those words. Firm, straightforward, and non-judgmental, polite exudes compassion and concern. Love-based vs. ego-centered, kind vs. crude – you decide.

Unless you are speaking the Word of God, your truth is shaded with personal experiences and issues, self-image, pain, insecurity, and some flawed beliefs. Speak kindly.

Affirmation: *"I speak from my heart and my words are tempered with kindness."*

Cheaper By the Dozen

"Seek revenge, get even, have an eye-for-an-eye mentality?" If anything is an affront to God it's vengeance. To me, there isn't a more senseless act humans engage in than getting even. "You hurt me – now you're going to pay!" To the best of my knowledge, no one has ever been ordained by the Almighty to seek retribution against one who sins. Remember, to sin is to miss the bull's-eye, the mark of perfection. Which of us has not fallen short of excellence? Revenge serves no constructive purpose. Humans, long thought to be the highest form of intelligence on the planet, are the only life form that seeks revenge. Maybe we need to rethink our position in the hierarchy of life or in our method of reprisal. Vengeance does not negate the transgression nor does it engender justice. The offense still is.

Many years ago I had the privilege of meeting Sister Helen Prejean, author of the highly acclaimed <u>Dead Man Walking</u>. In her argument against capital punishment she noted that in taking the life of the convicted, not only does it fail to restore life to the victim but additionally creates a second set of victims - the family of the convicted. "Oh well, too bad! The guy was scum and deserves to die!" But how does causing additional pain and suffering for the innocent (the family) promote justice? It doesn't.

"Well, if you don't want to do the time, don't do the crime." I agree there has to be some type of consequences but I also believe they must be within the dictates of God's Law. The Sixth Commandment does not come with an exemption clause - "don't kill except under the following conditions..."

Some continue to argue they have the right to teach others a lesson. Those who do wrong need to learn. We are all students of life but how do we learn best - through violence or love or by words or actions? Lessons are most effectively taught and learned by example. Living and loving as God does allows us to be teachers to all whom we encounter. God's way of healing - forgiveness and love - restores connectedness to Source and ultimately inner peace. His Way must be our way.

Affirmation: *"I pray for healing for those who have wronged me. I live to bring God's message to peace to the world."*

A Baker's Dozen

(This is the last one – I promise.)

"Allow others to take advantage of you, use or abuse you, to neglect you or disrespect you? Do you keep peace at all costs?" What pleases God is not simply how we treat others but equally as important is how we allow others to treat us. After all, we are His beloved children as well. I have a client who complains the reason she is mistreated is because she's *too nice.* She believes it's the way God expects her to be. She accommodates everyone's requests, allows others to treat her badly, and receives less than what she is rightfully deserving of. The world needs nice people but let's not confuse nice with passive or insecure. Too often, we allow others to take advantage of us because we are afraid to say "no". They might get angry, not like us, argue with us, break up with us or think we're not nice. Contrary to what many would have us believe, *nice-aholics* are deeply concerned about what others think and say about them and therefore comply with whatever transpires.

The perpetual people-pleasers, do-gooders, and peace-keepers - they are trodden upon by the world. They get stuck with the dirtiest jobs, are rarely appreciated for their efforts, and oftentimes work harder than anyone else. Sound like anyone you know? You were not created to be a doormat. God is not pleased. Be nice but expect respect.

Affirmation: *"I am confident with who I am. I deserve respect and recieve it."*

Breakfast of Champions

Wow – what a workout! Are you exhausted? I know I am.

I'm not going to belabor this section any longer. You get my point. Upon first glance, it is easy to deceive ourselves into believing we are righteous in God's eyes - "There's nothing wrong with me." You're right. Intrinsically, there is not one fiber of your being that is a mistake. But behaviorally speaking, there is enough to write a book about. Forgive me if you took offense to that statement but we all still have a lot of work to do on ourselves, including yours truly. I've come a long way but I have many more miles ahead of me. There is still plenty wrong with my behavior (ask my husband). My journey back to Spirit will continue until my time in this body has concluded.

A Bad Brake

Last week I took my car to my mechanic to have my tires rotated. After a few minutes, he emerged from the garage and exclaimed, "Janet, you have a real problem." *Who does he think he is*, I thought? I got really ticked off. "How dare you!" I shouted. "You ought to take a look at yourself in those filthy clothes! You're nothing to brag about!" Then I punched him in the face.

I find it amusing that we take such personal offense when someone points out a flaw they recognize in us. Rather than examine it for any shred of validity, we react defensively and dismiss their observations. If we could only get past our ego, we might discover something about ourselves we were previously unaware of. Then once the acknowledgment has been made, we can correct the imperfection and reap the benefits.

I grabbed my key and stormed out of Rob's Auto Shop. I never made it home. My brakes failed and I hit a tree coming around the bend on Berkshire Valley Rd. I broke my collar bone and have cuts and bruises all over my face. My car is totaled. Seems, my front brakes were shot. What a mess! If only I had listened…

Oh, no, don't get upset! I'm sorry - I made up that story to make a point. I'm fine and so is my car. But imagine if I had been so arrogant and defensive when someone tried to warn me something was wrong with my vehicle? Don't allow personal insecurities and ego to cause you to overlook a possible defect. None of us is perfect. Take a moment and check it out. It could make a huge difference in your personal well-being and maybe even save your life.

CHAPTER 9

The Road ~~Less~~ Almost Never Traveled Leads to Heaven

Eye of the Tiger

One of my favorite songs is "Eye of the Tiger" from an old "Rocky" movie. Sylvester Stallone (Rocky Balboa) needed to develop the *eye of the tiger* in order to become a championship boxer. While I am not a proponent of boxing per se, I do admire the commitment to remaining so focused on the prize that one almost acquires tunnel vision, never losing sight of his goal. Taking an *eye of the tiger* approach is precisely what is needed to transform one's life back to Spirit. One must be fully willing to forsake ego in every situation, no matter how tempting, and remain focused on making life-choices pleasing to God instead. Nothing and no one must deter us from living fully connected to Father. Being at one with the One must be our top priority at all times.

Prodigal Mother

Imagine, if you will, being abandoned by your mother as a child. For reasons unbeknownst to you, at age eight she left you and your younger siblings in the care of your father to raise by himself with no explanation or contact for years. Then one day, as a young adult with a family of your own, the phone unexpectedly rings. An unfamiliar voice offers a timid greeting. "Karen, it's your mother." *My "who", you think?* Your ears begin to buzz as you feel your knees weaken. "Who is this?" you query, voice skeptical with disbelief. "Your mother. I know you haven't heard from me in a long time but I've never stopped thinking about you. I want to be a part of your life," the woman confesses. Thoughts race wildly through your head as you struggle to select your response. Thirty-some years of repressed anger rears its ugly head as ego prepares to counter - "Where were you all these years? You didn't care about me and my brothers when we were little and needed you! Well, we don't need you now!" You struggle to prevent the tears from flowing. Pain hovers on the brink.

But a gentle hesitation interrupts action as Presence unlocks your heart. "Will your response please Me?" Presence asks. In one silent moment, Spirit reveals Divine answer and gently positions it upon your lips. "I've been hoping for your call," you reply. "Your grandchildren and I are anxious to get to know you". Prodigal mother, forgiven for past mistakes, is shown the heart of God through a wounded child's act of unselfish love. You forgo your own pain and choose instead to reflect God's Presence in that precise moment. *This* pleases God as you begin the process of re-embracing and healing family.

Father Knows Best

One of the greatest blessings (and challenges) in my life has been my marriage to my husband. While he is truly one of the nicest and kindest men I've ever known, our marriage is seriously lacking in some areas of great importance to me. (In other areas, let me add, it is overly abundant.) But for the first five months after exchanging our vows, I contemplated filing for divorce - not because there was anything wrong with him but because the marriage was not how I had envisioned it. No matter how much effort I put forth, it appeared doomed to be unfulfilling and disappointing in several critical areas. (I'm sure he had similar doubts as well. Then again, maybe not…chuckle!) However, we were brought together through Divine Intervention and God asked that I be with him. I wasn't sure why but my faith was enough to keep me there. Over time, it has been revealed to me what a sacred gift my marriage actually is. In each area that was lacking, God asked me to refrain from pressuring my husband to be what I wanted him to be and to give me what I thought I needed. He asked instead for me to love him exactly as he is and appreciate and celebrate his sacredness with my entire being. If there is anything *wrong* with him, God and he would work on it together. I needed to remove myself from that equation.

God continued: "Let me, your Heavenly Father, provide for you where he is unwilling or unable", He said. "Remove all expectations from him. I can and will grant everything you need - comfort, appreciation, recognition, and opportunity - everything. Remember the birds in the field? I provide for them and I love you at least as much." I did as God requested. I relinquished all requests and demands. I learned to truly appreciate who my husband is, to graciously accept what and when he is willing to give, and to be at peace when my requests are denied. I turn instead to Father who supplies all of my needs as He promised. This single shift in awareness released all anger and anxiety and replaced it with a deep sense of security and an even deeper love for Father. I have come to rely on God alone. I expect nothing from anyone anymore. Whatever I need is supplied by Father. He is my source of all. And each time He fulfills His promise, my love for Him intensifies.

> *Each day, I fall in love with God all over again for the first time.*

God placed me in what I thought was a deficient marriage. In essence, it has proven to be one of my most cherished gifts. We may not always get what we want in life but we certainly always get exactly what we need. Any path that leads to Oneness with the Divine is the right path. Father really does know best.

Off the Beaten Path

We've all had well-intended people who have offered us what they believed to be sage advice for having the amazing life we deserve. Bookstore shelves are brimming with paperbacks showing us how to find happiness. But happiness is a transitory moment - my children and grandchildren come for a visit and I'm ecstatic! But ten o'clock arrives and all head home. A melancholy settles in where enjoyment resided and I am deeply saddened. Spending time together as a family becomes increasingly more sporadic as years pass. I feel condemned to a life of misery interspersed with moments of bliss. *Not a very bright future*, I think to myself.

But not to worry - that's why we have life coaches who help us uncover our life's purpose and outline a course to fulfill it. I now know why God created me and I begin my pursuit of passion. That's what my life is really all about - purpose and passion, the reason why I was put here. Except, I've developed health issues that have made it impossible for me to continue my work. Or perhaps the economy has put a strain on my industry and I find myself unemployed. I have lost my purpose in life and retreat into depression. What now?

Thank God I listened to my friends and family who encouraged me to find the perfect someone to love and get married. But the hum of his car in the driveway ceases as he is laid to rest. I fall asleep to the sound of my own tears.

Each of these presumptions for creating a life of substance (as well as those mentioned in the beginning of this book) contains one major flaw that predisposes us to a life of suffering and failure - each is built on ego, the premise that my life is about me - how I feel, what I want, and what is good for me. Ego-living (remember Wayne Dyer's words - Edging God Out) leads to disappointment as nothing in life is sustainable indefinitely. Everything has a shelf-life - our friendships, bank accounts, material possessions, hobbies, and careers - everything. And each comes with its own unique set of conditions - vacations offer us a fun and relaxing getaway, weather permitting, then it's back to work Monday morning. Blackberries, computers, and video games are great sources of learning and entertainment – when they work. Good friends are a Godsend – as long as we don't have a fight that ends our friendship. Each, in their own way, adds value to our lives but they must never be the reason for our existence.

A God-centered life, however, is void of all conditions, restrictions, limitations, and disappointments. Seeking to be at one with God and to please Him in everything we do consistently rewards us for His Way is the way to happiness and success.

Spiritual GPS

On a recent trip home from my daughter's house, I somehow made a wrong turn only to find myself on an unfamiliar highway late at night. Not to worry - my son and his trusty GPS were riding shotgun. "I'll just punch in our location and my GPS will tell us how to get home." My mind transported me back to the first time I used a popular internet website to get directions to a location approximately twenty miles from my house. I typed in both the starting point and arriving destination and my computer delivered step-by-step directions. Instantly, I recognized an error - I was instructed to travel east on a particular roadway when I knew emphatically the town was west of where I lived. Thankfully, I decided not to follow that advice. I'm sure you can appreciate my skepticism in a hand-held device my son was asking me to rely on.

Sure enough, that tiny lady inside the GPS told us to travel south. "Chris," I said, "We need to be heading north. We have to go over the Tappan Zee Bridge." "It's taking us to a bridge," he replied. "Yes, but which one?" I asked. "I don't know but don't worry. All we have to do is go over the bridge and we'll be back in N.J." "Not necessarily," I stated. "There's a sign for the Whitestone Bridge. That will *not* take us anywhere near N.J.!" The tiny lady kept reassuring us she was *recalculating* our position which ultimately sent us in circles for more than an hour. Finally, I recognized a familiar sign and did a *Donald Trump* on her - "You're fired!" I shouted.

We have all put our faith and trust in well-meaning but sometimes misguided people who offer unsolicited advice. Some of us have even paid credentialed professionals to assist us in understanding and resolving the issues presently causing problems in our lives. I know I have. Sometimes the advice they provide for us is spot-on. Other times it has been worthless and still others have only made matters worse. When we seek advice and guidance from imperfect sources, we put ourselves at risk for errors. When we seek advice and guidance from the All-Knowing (*and abide by it*), we always remain on the true path, making moral choices and ultimately arriving safely at our destination – eternal salvation.

Converse with friends but follow your Spiritual GPS - God Pleasing System.

> "Trust in the Lord with all your heart and lean not on your own understanding. In all your ways acknowledge Him and He shall direct your paths." ~ Proverbs 3:5,6

Olympic Gold

Are you up for one final challenge? (Say yes, please? I knew you would. I had faith.) If you are really serious about transforming your life from ego to Spirit, making your life a journey towards knowing the heart and mind of our Creator, of truly living to please Him in any and every way possible, then you are ready for the ultimate test. Remember, we are here not only to know God but to be a reflection of His presence in this world. He is a God of Love, a God of Mercy, and a God of Healing. We are meant to be the same.

For the most part, we all display Divine qualities from time-to-time. And essentially, we decide when and with whom we will manifest God's Word. Ego picks and chooses. Spirit is impartial.

Speak only Truth - God's Truth, not yours or mine. Live only Truth – His Truth. There is no other.

Think about someone in your life who you are not particularly fond of, perhaps someone you've had a falling out with or maybe someone who's betrayed you. Are they currently in your life? Has the relationship been severed? Are they deceased but the grudge continues? Ask Father for guidance. "How do you want me to handle this situation? Do you want me to reach out and make amends? Do you want me to pray for them? Am I expected to reinstate them in my life? Is forgiveness in order?" Forgo your own impulses - put your anger, disappointment, judgments, and bitterness aside. Ask God what would please Him? Regardless of the answer, follow His command. Do not concern yourself with the outcome. He will not lead you astray. He will not require anything of you that is not in your best interest. Your obedience and love has pleased Him and you will be shown His favor.

By doing so, you have also made His presence known to the other party. In this way, your opponent is given the opportunity to know God's Love and hopefully allow Him to heal their pain as well. Offer them Divine Love in the form of forgiveness, kindness, generosity, compassion, and so on. Just offer it. If they accept, wonderful and if not, let it go. You planted the seed. Father of the Earth will nurture it as He nurtures all His creations and in time, His time not ours, it will grow.

Lord, I am a physical manifestation of your presence in this world. Let all who know me come to know You through me. Help me to live my life every day in a way that pleases

You for You alone are my Lord, You alone
are my God, You alone are my Savior.
Amen.

I can hear someone say, "But that's not easy!" No Shit-take mushrooms! Life is as easy or difficult as you make it. It's meant to be an amazing adventure of discovery and growth. When you live your life to please yourself you struggle. When you live your life to please God it is effortless.

Please God - you will not be disappointed.

CHAPTER 10

The Great Truth

Wow, this has been quite a journey, hasn't it? I cannot even begin to express my gratitude and appreciation for your taking the time to read my book. I trust and pray you are now ready and willing (because you certainly are fully capable) of transforming your life for now you know

The Great Truth

Your sole purpose in life is to come to know the heart and mind of God and exemplify it in the world.

Everything else will follow. Remember, it has always been between you and God (Mother Theresa).

> "Seek first His kingdom and righteousness and all these things will be added." ~ Matthew 6:33

Later, Alligator

I have truly enjoyed our time together. I'm going to miss you but like all good friends, let's keep in touch. You have my email. Don't be a stranger. Keep me posted. Let me know how and what you're doing. I really do care. Be a blessing to yourself and all whom you encounter.

> "I delight to do Thy will, O Lord, for I know Thy will for me is supreme good in my present and my future." ~ Psalms 40:8

Be a physical manifestation of God's presence in this world.

~

Peace and joy, my friend,

Janet

11/2/19 All Souls Mass - 10:00 am
11/4/19 Dealing w/ difficult people
pray for them
More objective - protects you - (don't take everything personally)